Praise for *I Can't Believe You Just Said That!*

"Ginger Hubbard is fresh, funny, and full of wisdom. Her advice is overflowing with God's instruction and grace."

—Lysa TerKeurst, president, Proverbs 31 Ministries

"There's a reason why the Bible speaks so often about our tongues. Who doesn't need help! Ginger's book will help all of us—children and parents—as together we learn how to season our speech with God's abundant grace."

—Bob Lepine, cohost, *FamilyLife Today*

"If you have been wondering how to get to the root of your child's struggle with their sin-nature, *I Can't Believe You Just Said That!* is the book you need. It should be a reference for every parent looking to instruct their child with biblical, Christ-centered wisdom. An encouraging, empowering must-read for every parent."

—Heidi St. John, mother of seven, author of *Becoming MomStrong* (Tyndale 2017), owner of The Busy Mom Blog

"Parenting is no joke! In fact, it's one of the hardest holy assignments God calls us to. So what do you do when your kids bring out the worst in you with their embarrassing, inappropriate, dishonest, or disrespectful musings? Hold your tongue and get this book!"

—Renee Swope, mom of three from nine to twenty-three; bestselling author of *A Confident Heart*; and former radio cohost, Proverbs 31 Ministries

"Start with the heart. Develop a plan. Implement training. The result? Beautiful speech. This book shows you how without just increasing the consequences. A powerful training tool that every parent will want to implement, one chapter at a time."

—Dr. Scott Turansky, cofounder, National Center for Biblical Parenting

"Kids bickering, back-talking, or blaming? Do you find yourself exasperated trying to correct your dear darlings' behavior when it comes to what comes *out of* their mouths? Ginger Hubbard has assembled a biblical handbook for teaching our kids to allow God to empower them to temper their tongues. If you long for a little piece of quiet in your home, this helpful resource is just the ticket. Highly recommended."

—KAREN EHMAN, PROVERBS 31 MINISTRIES SPEAKER
AND *NEW YORK TIMES* BESTSELLING AUTHOR OF
KEEP IT SHUT, WIFE AND MOTHER OF THREE

"For those who wish to truly keep a loving understanding of Scripture central in their child-raising practices, this book is an excellent choice."

—FOSTER W. CLINE, MD, COFOUNDER OF LOVE AND LOGIC
INSTITUTE, COAUTHOR OF *PARENTING WITH LOVE AND LOGIC*

"It's so easy to get caught up in addressing our kids' outward behavior rather than the heart issues that drive the behavior. Sometimes we need someone to lead the way and help us dig deep as Christian parents. Ginger Hubbard has done that with this book. If you're looking for help as it relates to whining, blaming, disrespecting, tattling, disobeying, lying, and manipulating, look no further. This is what you need!"

—JILL SAVAGE, AUTHOR OF *NO MORE PERFECT
MOMS* AND *NO MORE PERFECT KIDS*

"I absolutely loved reading Ginger Hubbard's *Don't Make Me Count to Three* when my firstborn was a toddler. Fast-forward nearly a decade, and I now have three school-age girls (and a toddler boy to boot). Ginger's new book could not have come at a better time in my parenting journey. With the same biblical wisdom that Ginger is known for, she lays out how to use your children's 'untamed tongues' to help draw their hearts to Jesus."

—ERIN ODOM, AUTHOR OF *MORE THAN JUST MAKING
IT* AND *YOU CAN STAY HOME WITH YOUR KIDS*;
CREATOR OF THE HUMBLED HOMEMAKER

"As a momma, my own soul was greatly fed as I read the life-giving teachings Ginger gracefully unpacks in this book. I came away from my snippet reading times feeling as if I had soaked for several days in deep biblical parenting study. I not only learned lessons to share with my herd of children, I learned lessons for my momma heart as well!"

—JAMERRILL STEWART, MOMMA OF 8; BLOGGER, YOUTUBER, PODCASTER AT LARGEFAMILYTABLE.COM

"Sharing from a wealth of experience, Ginger unpacks sound biblical wisdom mixed with practical ideas for addressing the most difficult areas of child training. We must be intentional with our words and Ginger helps us reach our children's hearts, set up a grace-filled plan for walking them through their everyday word choices, and encourages us each step along the way. I can't recommend it enough."

—JEN SCHMIDT, CREATOR OF BALANCING BEAUTY AND BEDLAM BLOG; (IN)COURAGE AUTHOR OF *JUST OPEN THE DOOR*; FOUNDER AND HOST OF THE BECOMING CONFERENCE

"Ginger Hubbard has written a must-read for every parent. In our culture where thoughtless words are the norm, she challenges parents to dare to parent again. Filled with real-life examples and practical advice, this breakthrough book raises the bar for biblically focused training."

—RACHAEL CARMAN, AUTHOR AND SPEAKER, RACHAELCARMAN.COM

"If you've got a little yeller, tattler, gossiper, whiner, or complainer in your house, this is the book for you. With humor and fresh insights, Ginger Hubbard gives you a better way to tame your child's tongue— and it doesn't involve a bar of soap. There are no platitudes here; instead, you'll get loads of practical advice. I highly recommend this biblically solid book."

—JENNIFER DUKES LEE, AUTHOR OF *THE HAPPINESS DARE* AND *LOVE IDOL*

"*I Can't Believe You Just Said That!* is an excellent resource for parents who are at their wits' ends (or soon to be). More than merely correcting behavior, Ginger Hubbard takes it that essential step further to help you, the parent, to reach the heart of your child. Both inspiring and practical, this book equips you to handle common challenges in parenting such as complaining, bickering, yelling, and more. A must-read and a wise resource you'll find yourself returning to over and over again."

—LISA JACOBSON, CLUB31WOMEN.COM

"It's not often I read a book on parenting and agree with 99.9 percent of everything I read, but in this case I did. I absolutely loved *I Can't Believe You Just Said That!* Ginger Hubbard has taken the issue of heart-oriented discipline and developed it better than any [other author] I have read."

—PASTOR REB BRADLEY, AUTHOR OF THE CLASSIC
BESTSELLER, *CHILD TRAINING TIPS*

"*I Can't Believe You Just Said That!* is a gem! As a mom of teenagers, Ginger provides the guidance and wisdom that I long to have. This book is biblical and practical and gives detailed solutions that will produce change in our homes. I highly recommend this book as a wonderful resource for all Christian moms!"

—COURTNEY JOSEPH, WRITER AT WOMENLIVINGWELL.
ORG, THE HOME OF GOOD MORNING GIRLS

"Ginger Hubbard shows parents how to effectively train a child to honor God with his or her words. She moves beyond *what they say* to *why they say it* to help parents know how to teach the biblical principles of God-honoring speech that will serve them well for a lifetime."

—SHARON JAYNES, AUTHOR OF *THE POWER OF A WOMAN'S WORDS*

"As parents, we've all cringed at inappropriate words spoken by our children. Whether your child tends to whine, complain, yell, or argue, this book will give you a biblical plan for positive change."

—ARLENE PELLICANE, SPEAKER AND AUTHOR OF *PARENTS RISING*

"Parenting is not for the faint of heart, and teaching our kids to control the tongue is among our toughest battles. Ginger Hubbard has guided us through the real-life verbal issues our kids face and made us feel normal in the process. I'm grateful for this important resource."

—LISA WHITTLE, AUTHOR, SPEAKER, FOUNDER OF MINISTRY STRONG AND THE 5 WORD PRAYERS DAILY PODCAST

"*I Can't Believe You Just Said That!* is a veritable toolbox containing precision tools of truth concerning the tongue-related issues shared by all humankind. I wish I could have had this on my shelf when my children were young."

—ANGELA O'DELL, AUTHOR, SPEAKER, VETERAN HOMESCHOOLER; ANGELAODELLBLOG.COM

i CAN'T BELIEVE YOU JUSTSAIDTHAT!

BIBLICAL WISDOM FOR TAMING YOUR CHILD'S TONGUE

GINGER HUBBARD

NELSON
BOOKS

An Imprint of Thomas Nelson

Published in Nashville, Tennessee, by Nelson Books, an imprint of Thomas Nelson. Nelson Books and Thomas Nelson are registered trademarks of HarperCollins Christian Publishing, Inc.

Thomas Nelson titles may be purchased in bulk for educational, business, fund-raising, or sales promotional use. For information, please e-mail SpecialMarkets@ ThomasNelson.com.

Unless otherwise noted, Scripture quotations are taken from the Holy Bible, New International Version', NIV'. Copyright © 1973, 1978, 1984, 2011 by Biblica, Inc.' Used by permission of Zondervan. All rights reserved worldwide. www.Zondervan.com. The "NIV" and "New International Version" are trademarks registered in the United States Patent and Trademark Office by Biblica, Inc.'

Scripture quotations marked NASB are taken from NEW AMERICAN STANDARD BIBLE', © The Lockman Foundation 1960, 1962, 1963, 1968, 1971, 1972, 1973, 1975, 1977, 1995. Used by permission.

Any Internet addresses, phone numbers, or company or product information printed in this book are offered as a resource and are not intended in any way to be or to imply an endorsement by Thomas Nelson, nor does Thomas Nelson vouch for the existence, content, or services of these sites, phone numbers, companies, or products beyond the life of this book.

ISBN 978-1-4002-0493-9 (eBook)
ISBN 978-1-4002-0444-1 (TP)

Library of Congress Control Number: 2017956396

Printed in the United States of America
HB 02.20.2024

In loving memory of
Nancy Wit,
one of my favorite role-model moms
and
in dedication to my favorite four,
Wesley, Alex, Hudson, and Jackson

CONTENTS

I Know You Didn't Just Say That!

"Mooommy, I want some juuuiiice!" *Whining*
"She was mean to me first!" *Blaming*
"You're stupid!" *Disrespecting*
"Tommy's not doing what you told him to do!" *Tattling*
"No, I'm not going to clean my room!" *Disobeying*
"I didn't take a cookie from the jar!" *Lying*
"You don't love me anymore!" *Manipulation*

What causes a child to speak such tender words as "I love you" or "You're the best mommy in the world" in one breath and say something terrible in the next? Before I had children, whenever I thought about my future family, I envisioned happy, well-mannered little darlings who always obeyed. The kid kicking and screaming in the restaurant? Not going to happen with mine. The kid reaching from the grocery cart, greedily grabbing everything within reach? Not my child. The kid throwing an obnoxious temper tantrum on the floor after being told he can't have the candy bar? Nope. The kid hitting his sister, because he wants the toy and she won't give it to him? No way. Boy, was I in for a rude awakening.

So what happened to all my plans for great parenting and well-behaved children? The stick turned blue. Twice.

I'm guessing I'm not alone in this. In short order I became the mom who was consistently taken aback when her kids spoke foolishly, whether it was in the form of whining, lying, or talking back. With an expression of shock, I would ask, "Why do you act like that?" It made no sense to me. I had instructed my children not to whine or lie or talk back, and I had administered consequences whenever they disobeyed. I did not understand why my plan was not working. Why did they continue to act like that? After a closer look at the Word of God, I realized I was asking the wrong question.

Jesus explained, "For the mouth speaks what the heart is full of" (Matt. 12:34). In other words, there is merit to the old saying, "What's down in the well comes up in the bucket." The apostle Paul confirmed, "For all have sinned and fall short of the glory of God" (Rom. 3:23). Because we are sinners, it is natural for us to manifest sin in the words we speak, so it should not surprise us when our children do the same thing. Even children with agreeable dispositions show their sinful hearts through the things they say.

Our sin does not begin with our mouths; it begins with our hearts. Thus, it is not sinful words that defile the heart, but a defiled heart that brings forth sinful words. An impure heart pumps sin, infects the body, and spews contaminated words from the mouth. While the words our children speak alert us to a problem, we must understand that the heart is where the words are conceived. It took me a while to catch on to this myself, so if this is new to you, don't worry. Let's dig into this more deeply together.

Jesus said, "For it is from within, out of a person's heart, that evil thoughts come—sexual immorality, theft, murder, adultery, greed, malice, deceit, lewdness, envy, slander, arrogance and folly" (Mark 7:21–22). The sin that shows up in our words comes from inside of us, and it starts sooner than we might think. King David proclaimed, "Surely I was sinful at birth, sinful from the time my mother conceived me" (Ps. 51:5). When we as parents truly grasp the origin of sin and the total depravity of man, we no longer question why our children sin. I slowly learned to quit asking, "*Why* does my child sin?" and began to ask myself, "*When* my child sins, how might I point him to the fact that he is a sinner in need of a Savior? How might I help him understand and live in the power of the gospel?"

> OUR SIN DOES NOT BEGIN WITH OUR MOUTHS; IT BEGINS WITH OUR HEARTS.

The responsibility of training our kids to walk in this transformative way can seem overwhelming at times. It can be tempting to convince ourselves that their flaws are just natural character traits or personality quirks for which we should extend grace and leave it at that. After all, the child is human, and humans sin through the things they say. But, while it is natural for children to verbally sin, God's Word confirms that this natural inclination to sin does not excuse parents from their

God-given responsibility to train them in what is right. We are commanded to "bring them up in the training and instruction of the Lord" (Eph. 6:4). We mustn't excuse our children's sins simply because they are natural expressions of the flesh, but we also mustn't expect our children to never sin. After all, they are sinners in need of grace, just as we are.

When children speak offensively, parents often respond in one of two ways: either we ignore the child, hoping he will outgrow it, or we administer some sort of consequence, hoping to put the fear of God in him. Both methods are ineffective because they fail to train and instruct. There are occasions when ignoring may seem more convenient for us. After all, it does take time to "start children off on the way they should go" (Prov. 22:6). Yet, to ignore a child who needs correction and guidance is to selfishly place our own interests above the interests and well-being of the child.

Consequences for wrong behavior have their place, but they are not a substitute for training and instructing. Administering consequences without following through with righteous training only teaches children one thing—there are consequences for sin. While that is an important lesson, an even greater lesson is to understand the higher calling of living in ways that are pleasing to God and bring him the glory he deserves. Our purpose in disciplining our children is not merely to teach them to avoid consequences, but to train and instruct them to honor God with their lives, that being "the way they should go."

Are you embarrassed by the words that come out of your child's mouth? Could it be that you have grown accustomed to ignoring verbal offenses or merely administering punishment? The Bible warns us against these sorts of tactics: "A child left undisciplined disgraces its mother" (Prov. 29:15). Our mission is to teach children what's right, not to shirk our parental responsibilities by ignoring them or to exasperate them by failing to follow through with godly counsel for right living.

We have approximately eighteen wonderful years to train our children in righteousness. If only we could view all their verbal offenses as precious opportunities to teach them, surely then we would respond righteously whenever these offenses present themselves. We wouldn't feel inconvenienced, angered, or frustrated when our children blow it. Instead, we would be thankful, joyful, and eager for the chance to point them to Christ and his power to transform lives. Throughout this book, we'll dive into God's Word together and learn how to effectively implement his great purpose and plan for parenting.

Confessions of a Flawed Mom

Like any mom, as I was just starting out, I wanted to be the best mom I could be for my children, which meant I wanted to be more than a cook, chauffeur, maid, counselor, doctor, referee, and disciplinarian (just to name a few of the roles moms play). I wanted to be the mom who molded character, built confidence, nurtured, trained, guided, and pointed her children to Jesus in every situation. I wanted to be a great mom while my children were growing up, and once they were grown, I wanted to be an old mom with no regrets.

Before I had children, I had heard horror stories about everything from the terrible twos to rebellious teens. I certainly did not want my children to become one of those stories, so what did

I do? I prayed, I studied my Bible, and I read parenting books. As avidly as I read "what to expect during pregnancy" books before I was even pregnant, I read "how to raise 'em now that you've got 'em" books months before my first child was born. I convinced myself that if I could just stay one step ahead, I would victoriously glide right through those stages, cross the finish line with a sigh of relief, and reap the rewards of perfect parenting.

Once I was in the actual throes of parenting, however, I quickly learned there is no such thing as perfect parenting. I learned that all children are sinners, all parents are sinners, and because we are sinners, we will all make mistakes, no matter how well studied and well prepared we think we are. I learned that self-reliance is a slippery slope that leads to failure followed by guilt, while complete dependency on Jesus for all things leads to grace and freedom—even when we mess up.

My propensity to mess up and mess up big became all too clear to me one day when my daughter Alex was around five years old. Alex loved playing barefoot outside, and one cold afternoon she asked if she could go outside. I knelt and made eye-to-eye contact with her, ensuring that she heard and understood my instructions (a tip from a parenting book). I explained that it was cold and told her to put on her shoes and coat before going out. I even took it a step further and had her repeat my instructions, eliminating all doubt that to put on the coat and shoes would be an act of obedience and to not put on the coat and shoes would be an act of disobedience (another tip from a parenting book). Alex dutifully recited the words, and I, satisfied, let her go and turned back to my housework.

About twenty minutes later, I took the trash outside and found Alex running around barefoot. Not only were her feet a bluish-purple color, but she had also ruined the bottom of her new pants, which were a little too long and dragged on the ground when she didn't wear shoes. I was livid, and I'm not very proud of how I responded. Before I confess, however, please allow me to back up and explain what my day had been like before the discovery of the bluish-purple feet and torn pants. Because we all know circumstances and emotions can play a huge part in our reactions.

That morning began with me waking to discover that there had been a power outage during the night, deactivating my alarm clock, which had been set for 6:00 a.m. It was 7:15. I had exactly forty-five minutes to brush my teeth, throw on clothes, get two kids under the age of eight dressed and strapped in the back seat of the car, zip through a drive-through for breakfast (because there was nada in the house), and make it for an eight o'clock appointment with our pediatrician. In an immediate state of panic, I bolted up and swung my legs over the side of the bed. My left foot landed in a puddle of dog pee. *Great. Just great.*

We pulled out of the driveway in record time, but by the time we left the Burger King drive-through, which was packed, we had exactly two and a half minutes before our scheduled appointment across town. Of course, I pulled onto the highway behind a Lincoln Town Car with an elderly blue-haired driver who obviously had absolutely nothing to do that day. I rolled my eyes, activated my left blinker, and began easing the car into the passing lane. I was about halfway over when a driver behind me quickly changed to the left lane and floored it, forcing me back into the right lane. He came very close to scraping the side of my car as he sped around us. *So impatient. The nerve of some people.* I caught a glimpse of the driver as he whizzed by and was completely appalled by what I saw. I slammed my hand down on the horn, startling my kids in the back seat.

My oldest asked, "What's wrong, Mom?"

"Well," I huffed, "that idiot who just passed us is trying to eat and drive at the same time, and he almost hit the side of our car. I almost dropped my hash browns."

With my heart still pounding and my nerves shot from the near accident, we walked into the doctor's office fifteen minutes late. I scanned the waiting room, and lo and behold, guess who was sitting in the far corner on the right reading a book to his toddler? My ex-boyfriend from high school.

Please understand. I was sporting faded sweatpants, an oversized T-shirt with a ketchup stain on the sleeve, flip flops, no makeup, and my hair pulled up in a chip clip. I froze, and my ex-boyfriend looked up just as my daughter blurted, "Mooom, I gotta go poo-poo!" Now, let me make it perfectly clear that I was in no way out to impress an ex-boyfriend from high school. But still.

We made it through our appointment, and on the drive home I compiled a mental list of all I still needed to do: clean the dog pee off the floor, set the chicken out to thaw, run the washing machine again because the clothes washed two days ago were never moved to the dryer, make a grocery list for tomorrow, and surf the Internet to see what my ex-boyfriend's wife looks like. Not that it mattered. But still.

Deep in thought prioritizing my to-do list, I didn't notice the squirrel dancing the typical neurotic jig of indecision in the middle of the road until it was too late. A sickening *thu-thump*. A regrettable glance in the rearview mirror. A cute little ball of fur, perhaps a mama squirrel on her way back to the nest to feed babies, or an adolescent squirrel crossing the road to meet Daddy for tree-hopping fun, now spastically flailing and flapping while suffering an agonizing death on the black asphalt.

Let's rehash: alarm clock failure, dog pee, close-call could-have-been-fatal car wreck, utter disgrace in the waiting room, and murder of an adorable squirrel family member. It was a lot to take in before ten o'clock in the morning. I reacted like any Jesus-saved, Southern-raised female would: I started crying.

Fast-forward one hour, around eleven o'clock in the morning, and we are back to the scene with Alex. I'm taking the trash out, and there she stands with bluish-purple feet and torn pants. Rather than responding calmly to her act of direct disobedience with loving instruction and discipline, I reacted emotionally with impatience and anger.

With one hand on my hip and the other adjusting the chip clip in my hair, I blurted out, "Alex, I told you to put on your shoes and coat before you went out! Now your feet are half frozen, and just look at what you've done to your pants! Your daddy works so hard to buy you these pants, and this is how you show your appreciation? You just see how fast you can get your tail in your room!"

With her bottom lip quivering and big tears on the brink of spilling over, she ran into the house and flung herself on her bed. I deflated, and guilt set in as I walked to her bedroom and found her crying into her pillow, teddy bear clutched to her chest. I had sinned against God and my little girl with my angry tirade, and it had broken her heart. And mine.

Circumstances and emotions can play a huge part in our reactions, but that doesn't make them any less sinful or hurtful. Where did I go from there? On my knees before God, asking for his forgiveness, and on the edge of my daughter's bed, asking for her forgiveness. And his grace came down.

In our parenting, we are not always going to get it right, but I have found that there are two things that drastically improve our ability to respond wisely, calmly, and effectively, regardless of circumstances and emotions: prayer and a plan.

> THERE ARE TWO THINGS THAT DRASTICALLY IMPROVE OUR ABILITY TO RESPOND WISELY, CALMLY, AND EFFECTIVELY, REGARDLESS OF CIRCUMSTANCES AND EMOTIONS: PRAYER AND A PLAN.

No matter what stage of life our children are in, the most important thing we can do for them is pray. Whether they're in diapers, danger, love, rebellion, or a convertible sports car, our most powerful and effective tool in parenting is fervent prayer over every aspect of their lives.

As flawed parents with a sin nature, there are times we are bound to blow it, make wrong decisions, let our children down, and fail them in more ways than one. There is one thing we can do, however, that will always reap fruit and never return void, and that's pray for them. Christian author Stormie Omartian said that being a perfect parent doesn't matter, but being a praying parent does.[1]

The most confident prayers we can pray are those that come directly from God's Word. To pray for our children from God's Word is to pray in harmony with God's perfect will for their lives. Rather than praying for what we want to happen, which can sometimes prove shallow and vain, praying directly from Scripture unleashes the wisdom and power of our mighty Lord.

It surrenders our foolish misconceptions of what we think is best by acknowledging and accepting that God's ways are not our ways. To pray from the Scriptures is to seek the will of the Father rather than our will as parents. "'For my thoughts are not your thoughts, neither are your ways my ways,' declares the LORD. 'As the heavens are higher than the earth, so are my ways higher than your ways and my thoughts than your thoughts'" (Isa. 55:8–9).

Once we understand and are committed to the importance of praying for our children, the next step toward improving our ability to parent calmly and effectively is to come up with a good plan of action. Having a plan in place can aid us in responding wisely rather than reacting foolishly. As an overwhelmed young mom who desired to rightly address the issues with which my children struggled, I read many parenting books by godly authors. My favorite was *Shepherding a Child's Heart* by Tedd Tripp. His Christ-centered approach to parenting was exactly what I longed for, and his book inspired me to reach past the outward behavior of my children and address the issues of the heart from a biblical perspective. As I read and reread his book, I thought, *Yes! This is exactly what I want to do!* But as situations arose with my children, I didn't know how to implement what I had read. I was motivated but not equipped. I knew *what* I wanted to accomplish, but not *how* to accomplish it. I found myself frustrated by my inability to practically apply what I had learned.

I decided I needed a practical plan of action for every behavior with which my children struggled, such as lying, whining, and tattling. It needed to be a plan I could refer to quickly and implement easily as a busy mom. I jotted down the behaviors that needed correcting, and I came up with a three-step plan for addressing each one. Step one consisted of asking the child two or three heart-probing questions to help reach past the outward behavior and pull out the root sin. Step two identified what specifically needed to be *put off* and why, explaining to the child what God's Word says about the behavior or attitude and what it could lead to. Step three examined what needed to be *put on* and showed the child how to replace wrong behavior and attitudes with right behavior and attitudes.

Before I had this plan of action, I often found myself relying on my own words and wisdom, rather than on God's Word and wisdom, especially when in the heat of the moment or distracted by other things. Frustrated that I did not know what to say or do when caught off guard, I would merely send my children to their rooms or administer some sort of consequence. Realizing that I was falling short of truly reaching their hearts, I stapled my quick-reference chart together, hung it in my kitchen, and found it a powerfully effective tool for addressing sinful behaviors from a heart-oriented, biblical perspective.

Before the chart, when my daughter tattled on her brother, a common response from me might have been, "Well, go tell your brother to come in here and I'll deal with it." That response, however, failed to deal with what was going on in her heart (delighting in getting her brother in trouble), what God's Word says about tattling, and what she should "put on" instead of tattling. Having a simple, yet well-thought-out plan of action right at my fingertips helped me to stay consistent and self-controlled in dealing with every behavior and attitude that needed correcting, and the difference it made in my children was radical.

I am ashamed to say that I walked right past my chart the

day I blew it with my daughter. I allowed circumstances and emotions to override my desire to lovingly discipline and train her in wisdom. I didn't take time to pray or point her to the transforming power of the gospel. Thankfully, our God is not only a God of forgiveness and grace, but also a God of atonement and restoration.

After I sought forgiveness for speaking to Alex so harshly, I set about handling her act of disobedience in a way that reflects the love of Christ. What a difference it made! Our conversation went something like this:

Me: Alex, honey, I told you to put on your shoes and coat before you went outside. Did you obey or disobey?

Alex: I disobeyed.

Me: God says things don't go well for those who disobey and that children are to obey their parents in everything because that pleases the Lord. How does God want you to obey?

Alex: All the way, right away, and with a happy heart. (This is something I read in several parenting books and taught my children at a very young age, as it is a simple, clear description of biblical obedience.)

Me: Sweetheart, I love you too much to allow you to disobey. (Then I followed through with a consequence.)

Clearly, this self-controlled biblical response was far more loving and effective than my initial emotional reaction. What if

I had asked my child if she obeyed or disobeyed and she said she obeyed, trying to avoid a consequence, or what if she refused to answer at all? Well, you'll just have to read the book to find those answers. It's all about prayer and a plan.

Breaking Down the Plan

Having a plan of action can make a positive difference in how we respond to a child's need for correction. Since every chapter in this book uses the same three-step plan of getting to the heart of behavior, reproving children biblically, and training children in righteousness in correlation with specific tongue-related struggles, it is imperative that we understand the biblical importance of each of the three steps.

Step 1: Getting to the Heart of Behavior

A wise parent will learn to move beyond her child's words by addressing the issues of the heart. After all, if the heart is reached, the behavior will take care of itself. We are told by Solomon, the wisest man who ever lived, that drawing out matters of the heart is no easy task. He stated, "The purposes of a person's heart are deep waters, but one who has insight draws them out" (Prov. 20:5).

Jesus came to earth possessing the holiness of God but faced the trials of man. Thankfully, he exemplified ways to get to the heart of behavior. Throughout Scripture, Jesus often asked questions whenever someone was caught in sin. He would ask a question in such a way that the sinner had to take his focus off the circumstances around him or the wrongdoings of others and place it on his own heart and motives. Jesus' questions caused people to evaluate themselves, which led to the realization of their own sin and need for the Savior. Parents do well to follow the example of Christ by asking heart-probing questions. In doing this, they help children recognize and take ownership for their sins, which in turn helps them realize their need for Christ.

Step 2: Reproving Your Child Biblically

In Matthew 18:15 God commands that we reprove those who are caught in sin. A biblical reproof exposes wrong by shedding light where there is darkness. But what does this look like on a day-to-day level? Fortunately, God has faithfully provided us with what to say and how to say it. We need not look any further than the infallible Word of God. Once we have determined the issue of the heart that drives the outward behavior, then we can address the offense in accordance with Scripture.

We know that "all Scripture is God-breathed and is useful for teaching, rebuking, correcting and training in righteousness" (2 Tim. 3:16). We also know it is wise to use Scripture versus the words of others, or even ourselves, because it is not our words but God's words that will penetrate the heart, convict the guilty, and promote change: "The Word of God is alive and active. Sharper than any double-edged sword, it penetrates even to dividing soul and spirit, joints and marrow; it judges the thoughts and attitudes of the heart" (Heb. 4:12). Because we are provided with "everything we need for a godly life" (2 Peter 1:3), we can rest assured that a parent's guide to dealing with an unruly tongue is Scripture. We just need to know where to look.

As busy moms, it can seem overwhelming to figure out just how to find the right scriptures and ask the right kind of heart-probing questions to help with the specific struggles our children face. Good news! After I made that quick-reference chart for myself, I developed it a bit further to help my fellow moms as well. If you're looking for a good starting point, one option is checking out my *Wise Words for Moms* chart.[2] It breaks down twenty-two common behaviors with which children struggle (such as lying, tattling, and whining), offers suggested heart-probing questions, and identifies scriptures for specifically addressing each one. The chart certainly shouldn't be a substitute for studying Scripture on your own, but let's face it, there are some days it's just easier to have the answer right in front of you. As an older mom who remembers what it was like to be a younger mom, I've simply done the homework for you. Consider it your cheat sheet when you're having one of those days and just need a little helping hand.

Once we have some applicable scriptures in mind, whether from the chart or from some personal study, we need to put them to use. God not only provides perfect words of wisdom, he also offers instruction in how to speak those words. Paul taught, "If someone is caught in a sin, you who live by the Spirit should restore that person gently" (Gal. 6:1). Scolding should have no place in reproving children. King Solomon warned, "A gentle answer turns away wrath, but a harsh word stirs up anger" (Prov. 15:1). A parent is ready to reprove her child biblically when she can speak in a normal tone of voice and with carefully measured words. Solomon confirmed, "The heart of the righteous weighs its answers, but the mouth of the wicked gushes evil" (v. 28). If needed, never hesitate to take a moment to gain self-control to avoid "gushing evil" while administering reproof.

I believe many parents speak harshly out of frustration in

not knowing how to handle wrongdoings. When my children were growing up, the times I found myself raising my voice in frustration were the times when I was acting in my own strength, grasping for some quick, man-made solution to "fix" my child. When I was living in the counsel of God, submitting to his plan for parenting by responding in accordance with his Word, I found that I was less frustrated and less likely to sin against God and my child. Having a plan in place helps parents respond assertively in love and with self-control. After all, it's hard to scream the Word of God at our kids.

Step 3: Training Your Child in Righteousness

Here is where many parents stop short. Most have no problem with reproving their children for doing or saying something wrong. Too often parents simply tell the child what he has done wrong, administer some sort of consequence, and then go about their business, satisfied that they have fulfilled their parental responsibility.

The Bible is clear that we are to do more than this.

We are to take it a step further and train our children in righteousness. It is never enough to tell kids what not to do; we must teach them what to do. In the book of Ephesians we are told to "put off your old self, which is being corrupted by its deceitful desires; to be made new in the attitude of your minds; and to put on the new self, created to be like God in true righteousness and holiness" (4:22–25).

Teaching children to "put off" wrong behavior comes naturally for parents, mainly because we find wrong behavior unpleasant, but the key to successful parenting is found in training them in righteousness. It is equally important, if not more important, that we teach our kids what to put on when we tell them what to put off. This is what training them to walk in the righteousness of Christ is all about.

We must teach them how to replace what is wrong with what is right, or we will exasperate them. Paul warned, "Fathers, do not exasperate your children; instead, bring them up in the training and instruction of the Lord" (Eph. 6:4). There is a difference between disciplining with consequences and training with instruction. Administering consequences without following through with instruction leaves children with no means of escape. They learn what not to do, but they have nowhere to go from there. "God is faithful," Paul said. "When you are tempted, he will also provide a way out so that you can endure it" (1 Cor. 10:13). It is the parent's duty to offer a biblical alternative to the wrong behavior in order to provide the child with a means of escape.

> IT IS NEVER ENOUGH TO TELL KIDS WHAT NOT TO DO; WE MUST TEACH THEM WHAT TO DO.

TAMING THE TONGUE

As we begin this journey together following the three steps—getting to the heart, reproving biblically, and training in righteousness—there will be times when we will hit bumps in the road and become discouraged. But take heart! It is a worthwhile goal that we pursue. For such a small part of the body, the tongue holds great power. The apostle James made several interesting comparisons with this small, yet significantly influential part of the body. He likened it to a horse's bit. It is astonishing how a pocket-sized piece of metal placed into the mouth can guide such an enormous animal. James also equated the tongue with the rudder of a ship. Although diminutive in comparison to the size and weight of a ship, the rudder steers, taking the ship wherever the captain commands. After making these remarkable comparisons, James said, "Likewise, the tongue is a small part of the body, but it makes great boasts" (James 3:5).

It is impossible for you to manage your child's tongue. James said, "No human being can tame the tongue" (v. 8). It is possible, however, for you to help your child understand his need for Christ and the regenerative power of the gospel in his life. Because it is God's Word and God's Spirit that reveal these things, the foundation of our instruction must derive from Scripture. Paul said, "So the law was our guardian until Christ came that we might be justified by faith" (Gal. 3:24). Once your child understands his need for Christ and his heart is being governed by the Holy Spirit, he will begin to understand the sins of the tongue and his dependency on Christ for victory over those sins.

One thing we should guard against, though, is the dangerous mentality of *If I can just get my child to accept Christ, he will be good.* Not only is the work of the Spirit an ongoing labor after salvation, but the parents' effort to discipline and disciple their children in the truths of the gospel is ongoing as well. Our goal is not for our children to become Christians so they will "be good." Our goal is to lead them to Christ and help them understand that God alone is good, and it is only through his atonement that we can be seen in such a way.

To aid our kids as they grow and come to a deeper

understanding of the heart change Christ alone brings about, we as parents have the awesome responsibility of bringing them up in the discipline and instruction of the Lord. This book is designed to help you do that. Each chapter opens with a common, relatable scenario regarding a specific tongue-related offense, points out the root sin of the heart behind the outward behavior, and follows up with a three-step plan for addressing the issue: how to ask heart-probing questions, how to reprove your child (specifically what to *put off*), and how to train and encourage your child (specifically what to *put on*). Actual parent–child dialogue is included in every chapter as examples of the practical application. It is my deepest desire that this book motivate you not only in *what* to do, but also in *how* to do it.

If you find yourself falling into the traps of ineffective discipline, such as threatening, repeating your instructions, or raising your voice; if you are frustrated because it seems that no matter what you do or say, you just can't reach your child's heart; if you lay your head down at night and feel guilty about the way you parent; if you long for an easy-to-follow practical plan of action to help you stay on track; if you want to raise happy, content children who enjoy the rewards of self-controlled, obedient living, then keep reading. Throughout this book, you will find the tools you need to move past the frustrations of not knowing how to handle tongue-related issues of disobedience and into a confident and well-balanced approach to raising your children. It's all about prayer and a plan.

Lord Jesus, we thank you so much for the children you have entrusted to our care. It is our desire that we be tools, used by your hands, to whittle away the calluses of the heart so that our children will be tender and suscep-tible to you, your Spirit, and your truth. We know that true wisdom comes only from you. We ask that you grant us the wisdom we need to point our children to their deep need for you.

Lord, help us to not walk in condemnation when we blow it, but convict us when we sin against you and against our children. Lead us in how to humbly make things right so that you will be glorified in our weaknesses. Use our failures as a means for us and our children to bet-ter understand your forgiveness and grace.

Lord, we acknowledge that your ways are perfect and are higher than ours. Thank you for your Word and your Spirit, which has provided us with everything we need for life and godliness. May we never rely on ourselves, but always seek you, praying and petitioning for your work to be done in and through us. Prompt us in how to pray for our children in accordance with your plan and purpose for their lives. May they grow in knowledge and insight and be able to discern your good, pleasing, and perfect will. Give them a hunger, a thirst, and a deep love for you and your Word that they would desire you above all things.

You alone are worthy of all praise and honor. Bless our desires and efforts to raise our children in your ways that you will be praised and honored in our lives and theirs.

To you be the glory forever and ever, amen.

WHINING

It starts at six in the morning. "Mooommyyy, I don't wanna wear that shiiirt," whines Robin.

"But it looks so nice on you," Mom replies.

"But I don't wanna weeear iiit," Robin cries.

"Well, you're going to wear it anyway!" barks Mom.

The tantrum begins. It continues through breakfast.

"I don't like grape jellyyy," whines Robin.

"Since when do you not like grape jelly?" Mom asks.

"I want the straaawberryyy," Robin complains.

"Okay, I'll get the strawberry jelly," says Mom with a sigh.

"I'm thirsty. I want some juuuice," Robin begs.

"I'll get you some apple juice in a minute," Mom assures.

"But I want juice nooow," pleads Robin.

It drags on in the grocery store and continues in the checkout line. As Mom loads groceries onto the conveyer belt, Robin spots a ladybug stuffed animal on the shelf beside her.

"I want the ladybuuug," Robin demands as she reaches from the grocery cart.

"No, Robin, we aren't buying any stuffed animals or toys today. And I told you not to grab things from the shelves!" Mom retorts.

Robin strains and grunts as she continues to reach for the stuffed animal. Pushing the grocery cart away from the shelf, Mom ignores Robin's whimpering. Robin grows angry from the lack of attention and begins to wail.

Embarrassed and desperate for Robin to quiet down, Mom yells through clinched teeth, "Stop that whining right now, Robin, or you're going to get it!"

Another tantrum.

Mom backs up, grabs the stuffed animal, and hands it to Robin, hoping she will stop screaming.

Understand the Heart of the Matter

Is there anything more annoying than whining? Perhaps, but off the top of my head, I cannot think of it. Children who whine lack healthy communication skills. Parents must not blame the child for this behavior. Rather, they must understand that children whine simply because they are allowed to whine. Therefore, the fault lies not with the child, but with the parent. Parents are often responsible for their children's habits. Moms and dads who permit their children to whine (by ignoring or giving in) keep them from learning to communicate appropriately in a way that pleases God. The bad news is that when we allow our children to whine, it not only hinders others from enjoying their company, but also hinders our children from enjoying life. The good news is that no matter how accustomed your child is to whining, he or she can learn to communicate properly.

Children who use demanding forms of communication to express their wants and needs are in bondage to their emotions and lack of self-control. An enslaving addiction to whining does not make for a happy child (or parent). Children who learn to communicate properly, however, learn that self-control is a prerequisite for contentment, joy, and good living. Some may assume the Bible does not address whining or how to handle it, but if we look past the outward behavior and seek to address the heart issue, we understand that whining is an issue of self-control. And God has a lot to say about self-control.

He compares a person who lacks self-control with a city whose walls are broken down (Prov. 25:28). He deems self-control so important that he lists it as a priority virtue (Gal. 5:22–23). He says that we are "to say 'No' to ungodliness and worldly passions, and to live self-controlled, upright and godly lives in this present age" (Titus 2:12).

God's commands are for his glory and our joy. Honoring him by speaking with a *self-controlled voice* accomplishes both purposes. God is glorified when we obey his commands, one of which is to live self-controlled lives. When we choose to obey his commands, he puts joy in our hearts, which reflects his own joy of being glorified. We've all witnessed the lack of joy a whining child demonstrates versus the joyful countenance of a child who has been taught to communicate with self-control. We must understand that biblical instruction is for the good of God's children. In giving reasons for us to obey his commands, Jesus said,

"I have told you this so that my joy may be in you and that your joy may be complete" (John 15:11). He always desires to enable us, through his power, to follow his commands, which brings joy to his children.

Age-Appropriate Communication

You may be questioning if words such as *self-control* are too difficult for a young child to understand. While you certainly do not have to verbally correct and train the same way I do throughout this book, I encourage you to use biblical terminology as much as possible, especially when it comes to identifying specific sin issues and God's commands for his children. Our goal is for our children to know the Word of God and have it firmly tucked into their hearts as early as possible. Just as infants do not know that Mommy and Daddy are the faces smiling down at them unless those faces repeat the words over and over, a small child will not relate to the Word of God unless it is repeated to them over and over. Children learn and relate to words by hearing them *in the context of the moment.*

> The sooner children are taught the Word of God, the sooner they begin to understand the wisdom and power it offers for their lives.

I mentioned this in chapter 1, but I believe it is important to reiterate here. It is wise to use Scripture because it is not our words but God's words that penetrate the heart, convict the guilty, and promote change. As Paul said in the book of Hebrews, "The word of God is alive and active. Sharper than any double-edged sword, it penetrates even to dividing soul and spirit, joints and marrow; it judges the thoughts and attitudes of the heart" (4:12). The sooner children are taught the Word of God, the sooner they begin to understand the wisdom and power it offers for their lives.

One of the most common questions asked at my conferences is "When is my child old enough to learn to obey?" My answer is "A child is old enough to learn to obey when he is old enough to disobey." When are children old enough to begin understanding God's Word? As soon as they are old enough to violate God's Word, and as soon as they are old enough to find themselves in situations where they need the wisest encouragement and counsel—which comes only from God's Word. Perhaps the most important reason of all to start using biblical language early is that it is the living and active Word of God that teaches us our need for Christ.

Now, having said that, don't exasperate your children by overdoing verbal correction using biblical terminology. Use God's Word, but keep it simple, short, and in accordance with the specific issue at hand. When children whine, it is a great opportunity for them to relate God's desire for them to have self-control with the biblical word. When you use words such as *self-control* and *obeying* in the context of their behavior, they begin to relate the Word of God to their lives. This is our goal. But avoid launching into a ten-minute sermon using every verse you know on the topic. Young children have short attention spans, as do many teenagers for that matter. Try to keep in mind that enough said is enough said.

Ask Heart-Probing Questions

When the issue of whining arises, take that first step of our plan and ask your child if she is speaking with a self-controlled voice. This helps her to take ownership for her own behavior. You might ask, "Sweetheart, are you asking for juice with a self-controlled voice?" Granted, she may not answer. Even if she doesn't, however, you have still helped her to evaluate her heart and consider her own lack of self-control. She will ponder the answer, even if she refuses to verbalize it. If she shrugs instead of answering, gently speak the truth on her behalf: "No, you were not asking with self-control."

Reprove Your Child for Whining

As we move on to reproving, it is important to speak calmly. Whining can certainly get under the skin. A mom who responds to whining by yelling, "Stop that whining right now or you're going to get it!" is training in anger and not modeling the self-control that she so desperately desires her child to learn. Also, when correction is administered in anger, the child will view it as a personal attack or an act of vengeance, rather than careful instruction given in love. Correcting wrong behavior should never come out of an "I'll show you" or a "Boy, you're going to get it now" mentality. It should be given with an attitude of "I love you too much to allow you to live an undisciplined life."

Don't overdo your reproof. You might simply say, "Honey, God wants you to have self-control, even with your voice. Because you need to learn to speak the right way, I will not discuss this while you are whining." Explain to her that God commands her to have self-control (Titus 2:12), and that when she asks him for it, he will give it to her in accordance with his command. You might say, "Sweetie, did you know God will help you to speak with self-control if you ask him?"

While I try to provide scriptures to support suggested dialogues throughout the book, that doesn't mean you must reference where the scriptures are found every time you communicate God's truths to your children. It's good for children to begin memorizing Scripture young, but it's also good to bring the truths of God's Word into natural, everyday conversations. For the sake of maturity level and attention span, I found it more effective to keep instructional conversations casual and short rather than long and preachy.

Train Your Child to Speak with Self-Control

Once we have explained to our kids the biblical reasons to speak without whining, we can move on to training in righteousness. As a consequence for whining, have your child wait three minutes before asking again. Three minutes can seem like an eternity for a small child. Be sure to explain that it is love that motivates you to train her. You might say, "Sweetheart, I love you too much to allow you to speak foolishly. Because I want to help you learn to speak with self-control, I'm going to set the timer for three minutes." (You could use a kitchen timer or stopwatch.) Then explain, "When the buzzer goes off, you may ask for juice the right way." It may be necessary to demonstrate the correct way to speak to help your child along. By requiring her to ask the right way, you are correcting what she did wrong, but, even more important, you are training her in what is right.

If the child refuses to ask the right way after the three-minute consequence, perhaps deciding she doesn't want the juice after all or as an act of stubbornness, don't force her to ask again when the buzzer goes off, as that can encourage a power struggle. Simply don't offer the juice, and let it go. This provides a natural consequence to her defiance. The next time she does ask for juice (or something else) in a whiny voice, however, repeat the heart-probing questions, reproof, and requirement to ask the right way before you respond to her request.

When to Use This Method and When Not to Use This Method

This method is effective for teaching children who ask for things in whiny voices as well as for children who use whiny voices as a general means of communicating. For example, if a child says in a whiny voice, "I don't like that color" or "My doll stroller isn't rolling right," she's not necessarily asking for something, but she is inappropriately communicating her thoughts and feelings. Whining in this case is simply words spoken with a bad attitude, which also reflects a lack of self-control. Don't indulge the child by responding to her topic, but guide her to an acceptable form of communication.

Begin with the same sort of question, "Are you talking with a self-controlled voice?" Let her know that "Mommy will only talk about this with you if you speak with self-control." Then follow through with biblical reproof and training in right communication, again, modeling it for her if necessary.

If your child asks for something with a self-controlled voice and the answer is no and *then* the child whines, you have an issue of disrespect and defiance on your hands. This is not the time to have her ask again but to administer consequences. After consequences, however, I encourage you to walk the child through how she *should have responded* to your answer (see chapter 5 on defying). Once again, this is teaching her how to replace what is wrong with what is right. It is offering her that "means of escape" and preparing her to respond appropriately to future situations that are similar.

It's Never Too Late

Perhaps you have allowed your child to develop a habit of whining by either giving in or ignoring the problem. Please be encouraged that it is never too late to train your child to communicate properly. Begin your transition to the new training by asking for your child's forgiveness. You might say, "Sweetheart, it's my job to teach you how to speak with self-control, but I have been allowing you to whine. Will you forgive me for not teaching you how to speak the right way?" Explain to your child that while whining has been accepted in the past, it will not be accepted anymore.

Be consistent in training, never give in to whining, and follow through with this plan every time an opportunity presents itself, and you'll have a whine-free life (and a more joyful, self-controlled child) before you know it.

A Deeper Look at Whining

Children who whine as a general means of communicating or to express their God-given needs, such as being thirsty, hungry, or tired, simply need to be encouraged in how to express those thoughts and needs with self-control, which is what has been addressed in this chapter. When left unchecked, however, children who continue to whine, demanding that their wants and desires be immediately met, can easily be led into the deep-rooted sin of idolatry. Their whining arises from the idolatry of selfishness, which believes that wants and desires take precedence over everything else and that their souls can be satisfied by immediately attaining those wants and desires. It involves a turning away from satisfaction in the Creator and takes on a selfish yearning for temporal pleasures as a substitute for finding rest and contentment in God.

Now, bear with me. I am not encouraging you to prop your three-year-old on your lap and engage in a lengthy conversation about the sin of idolatry and expect him to understand. However, as parents we do need to recognize this sin in our children (and ourselves), and as our children grow and mature, we need to help them recognize it as well.

The apostle Paul talked about those who substituted the temporal for the eternal. He said, "They exchanged the truth about God for a lie, and worshiped and served created things rather than the Creator—who is forever praised" (Rom. 1:25). We know that God "richly provides us with everything for our enjoyment" (1 Tim. 6:17), but those gifts for our enjoyment become idols when they are desired and enjoyed over God himself. A good indicator that gifts are becoming idols is when the absence or withholding of them ruins our trust and delight in the goodness of God.

There is nothing wrong with enjoying the temporal pleasures God grants us, but when we see them as a right and demand to enjoy them, then those pleasures become idolatrous. When idolatry takes place, God becomes jealous. In regard to idols, God said, "You shall not bow down to them or worship them; for I, the LORD your God, am a jealous God" (Ex. 20:5). God's jealousy is both righteous and loving. In his righteous jealousy, he deserves our deepest and strongest affections. In his loving jealousy, he created his children to find their greatest joy and satisfaction in seeking him as their greatest treasure. This is why Paul warned, "Therefore, my dear friends, flee from idolatry" (1 Cor. 10:14).

When your child is constantly whining for something, encourage her to love and desire God above all else. As she matures, and at an age-appropriate level of communication, you will want to go one step further and help her understand that only a deep soul satisfaction in God will give her the power to set aside her demands and her all-consuming, insatiable hunger for the next thing. It is essential that she understands that she is a sinner with a restless soul in search of satisfaction. She needs to grasp that sin alienates her from God and sends her in a restless and demanding search for satisfaction elsewhere.

Again, most chronic whiners are younger and will not easily grasp the concept of how idolatry and self-centeredness are at the heart of their whining. Therefore, it may be best to simply address the issue of self-control as laid out in this chapter while they are young. As they mature and you begin teaching the deeper issues, the all-powerful truth of God's Word will penetrate their hearts, and, accompanied by the Holy Spirit, it will bring about an understanding that we cannot convey on our own.

As your child matures and you begin warning her against the dangers of idolatry, you might simply explain, "Honey, idolatry is when a person or thing is loved more than God, wanted more than God, desired more than God, treasured more than God, or enjoyed more than God. Nothing can satisfy us more than God, which is why we are warned in the Bible, 'Dear children, keep yourselves from idols'" (1 John 5:21).

The good news is that whining provides a valuable opportunity to teach your child to communicate with self-control and, more important, to show your child her need for the grace of the gospel that delivers her from the deep-rooted sin of idolatry.

LYING

Mom notices a cookie-crumb trail leading from the kitchen to Zach's room. When Mom opens the door, Zach stops chewing, turns away from Mom, and takes interest in a toy truck.

"Zach, I told you not to get a cookie," Mom reminds.

"I didn't get a cookie," Zach responds around the cookie in his mouth.

Mom walks over and turns Zach to face her. Wiping the chocolate-chip smear from his cheek, Mom asks, "You have the cookie in your mouth right now, don't you?"

Zach furrows his eyebrows in determination. "No, I don't!" he retorts as crumbs spew from his mouth.

UNDERSTAND THE HEART OF THE MATTER

Why do children lie? For that matter, why do any of us lie? According to the book *The Day America Told the Truth*, 91 percent of those surveyed in a national survey on private morals admitted to lying on a regular basis.[1] The other 9 percent were probably lying. Though this survey was conducted in the nineties, we probably haven't changed that much since then. We still exaggerate details in our favor, twist the truth to make ourselves look good, hide facts to protect our guilt, and embellish stories to enhance our good image. No matter the form or extent, lying derives from the love and preservation of self. Children are no different. They are smaller versions of us. Like us, they will even deny the obvious to save face and avoid consequences.

The precocious child is clever with lies and may hone in on exact wording. He finds his justification and escape through twisting words in his favor.

Mom calls home while running errands. "Corey, did you remember to pick up your dirty clothes from the floor and put them in your laundry basket?"

"Yes," Corey responds.

Mom arrives home twenty minutes later. In gathering laundry baskets from the bedrooms, she finds Corey's clothes scattered on the floor. "You told me you remembered to pick up your clothes!" Mom fumes.

Corey pauses, then replies, "Yes, I remembered as soon as you called. But then I forgot again as soon as we hung up."

Not only has Corey justified the lie in his head, but he is also trying to manipulate Mom into believing he is innocent. Nice try.

In addition to blatantly dishonest statements like this, lying can take on various other forms, many of which seem not so bad in comparison. Do not be deceived. Sin is sin, and wrong is wrong. Because Christ died for our transgressions, none are small. The price he paid was great. To brush off any sin as being minor, or to trust that the crossing of fingers behind a back somehow lessens immorality, is a slap in God's face. All lies count as an offense against God, no matter the motive, rationalization, or hokey, superstitious attempt at atonement. In other words, the child who tells a half truth is just as guilty as the one who tells a full-fledged lie. The child who exaggerates a true story is just as guilty as the one who concocted the entire tale. Blatant deceit, half truths, and exaggerations are all the same in the Lord's eyes.

Even "white lies" that seem easily justified as necessary are a sin in the Lord's eyes. God tells us to be truthful. To make our own exceptions to his command is to believe ourselves wiser than God. Regardless of form, lying expresses a lack of love for God and a lack of trust that he is in control. Lying is always an attempt to bring about the response or outcome of our choosing—one that suits our own interests. It is to try and take on the duty of altering the natural response or outcome, which places the one who is lying in a position of control.

> LYING IS ALWAYS AN ATTEMPT TO BRING ABOUT THE RESPONSE OR OUTCOME OF OUR CHOOSING—ONE THAT SUITS OUR OWN INTERESTS.

When our daughter was three, she lied about doing something she was forbidden to do by blaming the deed on a small toy action figure. When I tried to logically reason with her that a three-inch toy man was not capable of doing such a thing without her help, she calmly argued that it was batteries that enabled her plastic friend to act on his own free will—and oh, how she tried and tried to warn him! She told him not to do it because it's wrong to disobey, but he did it anyway. Pretty clever for a three-year-old.

To be completely honest with you, it was hard not to laugh at her fabricated story. She was so cute with her little blond ponytail bobbing up and down and her hands on her hips as she confessed in great detail the dirty deed of the caped hero. Sin is not a laughing matter, however. We shouldn't chuckle or make light of the things for which God sent his Son to die.

We also shouldn't soften sin by making it sound less offensive than it is. We tend to call a small lie a *fib*, a big lie a *doozie*, and a "necessary" lie *white*. Somehow, these softer terms make them seem less wrong and more justifiable. Whether it is an intentional deceit, a slight exaggeration, or a half truth, lying is wrong in the eyes of the Lord. In fact, it is so wrong that God lists a "lying tongue" second among the seven things he hates (Prov. 6:16–19).

God hates the evil of lying. Because he is the Father of truth, he cannot lie or condone lying of any kind. When Thomas asked Jesus how to know the way, Jesus answered, "I am the way and the truth and the life" (John 14:6). While God is the Father of truth, Satan is the father of lies. In describing Satan, Jesus said, "When he lies, he speaks his native language, for he is a liar and the father of lies" (8:44). What makes this statement sobering on a personal level is what Jesus said in the first part of the verse: "You belong to your father, the devil, and you want to carry out your father's desires." Granted, Jesus was talking to those who were not his children, but children of the Devil. However, the reality is all children want to please their father. When children lie, they are following and pleasing the father of lies, Satan. When children are truthful, they are following and pleasing the Father of truth, God.

While following and pleasing our heavenly Father are reasons enough to speak truth, there are also relational consequences when children choose to lie. A solid foundation for all family relationships is trust. When trust is violated, relationships crumble. Honesty is the glue that holds a family together. When dishonesty oozes in, the glue loosens and the bond of trust falls apart. We are wise to adhere to Paul's advice: "Do not lie to each other" (Col. 3:9). In regard to being members of one family, Paul also penned, "Each of you must put off falsehood and speak truthfully" (Eph. 4:25). Because of God's desire to transform us into his likeness, as well as his desire for families to remain faithful and united to one another, he reiterates the importance of being truthful over and over throughout Scripture.

Ask Heart-Probing Questions

Back to the cookie scenario. Little Zach has been caught red-handed, but rather than admitting he ate the cookie, he blatantly lies. As his parent, you might start the process with, "Sweetheart, do you know who the father of lies is?" If he doesn't answer, offer guidance. "Satan is the father of lies. God is the Father of truth. Do you think lying honors God and your family?" He will ponder these questions and begin thinking from a biblical perspective even if he does not verbally answer.

Reprove Your Child for Lying

Next, explain how lying damages family relationships and how God hates a lying tongue. You might say, "Not only does

God hate a lying tongue because it dishonors him, but family relationships are built on trust. When you lie, trust in the relationship is broken. It is important that we keep trust in our relationship and that we honor God by being truthful. The Bible says that one of the seven things God hates is a lying tongue (Prov. 6:17). We 'must put off falsehood and speak truthfully'" (Eph. 4:25).

Train Your Child to Speak Truth

As you move on from reproving to training, you might say, "In Proverbs we are told that the Lord delights in those who are truthful [12:22]. Sweetheart, when I asked if you had a cookie in your mouth, what should you have said that would have been truthful?" Requiring him to practice telling the truth is training him to walk in the righteousness of Christ, rather than just reproving his sin.

A Word of Warning

To merely punish a lying child will do more harm than good. What we deem as "I am punishing you because you lied," the child deems as "You are punishing me because you found out the truth." As a result, they will only become better liars.

Another dangerous response is anger, which will cause him to fear ever telling the truth. It is best to calmly address the relational consequences of lying, admit our own struggles with lying, and encourage a total dependency on Christ, who is our only hope for redemption and change. It is a self-controlled, transparent, and gospel-oriented response to a lying child that will pave the way for more honest communication.

When you are certain that your child has lied, it is also more beneficial to address the fact that he lied, rather than calling him a liar. In calling him a liar, you are labeling him a liar, rather than encouraging him to live in the forgiveness and atonement of Christ. When my children were caught red-handed in a lie, I aimed to keep them focused on who they were in Christ by saying something such as, "Alex, you told a lie, but you are not a liar. That is not who you are. You are a forgiven child of God, and because of his grace, you can walk in truth." The best thing a parent can do is to take every opportunity to point their children to Christ and his power to transform lives.

We must be careful to model honesty ourselves. Statements such as "Just tell them I'm not home" when the phone rings, or "Of course the Easter bunny is real," or "Your goldfish swam down the toilet, through the pipes, and into the ocean, where he will enjoy happily ever after with Nemo" don't cut it in the honesty department. Whether the lies are on-the-spot obvious or later exposed, they cause the child to question the significance of the line between honesty and dishonesty. If we are not careful, we can ruin our credibility and instill a confusing distortion of reality, which may set your child back on his path to learning more honest communication.

ERR ON THE SIDE OF MERCY WHEN UNCERTAIN

If there is any question as to whether your child is lying, I encourage you to err on the side of mercy. Sir William Blackstone coined the saying, "Better that ten guilty persons escape, than that one innocent party suffer." To be accused of lying when, in fact, the child is telling the truth can be devastating. He could perceive that you have an ongoing, suspicious expectation of him lying, which will discourage him. If your intuition is that your child is lying but you are uncertain, pray that God would bring it to light so that you might have the opportunity to point him to the atonement of Christ.

Don't stress over the possibility that your child has gotten away with a lie because of your uncertainty. If he is given to lying, he will lie again in a situation where you are certain, giving you the opportunity to train him in truth. My friend Rick told me of a time when his son got away with a lie:

> I remember when one of our boys was about ten. There was a situation where he insisted that he was innocent. While it didn't seem that way to me, I was uncertain, so I let it go. Weeks later during the middle of a family devotional, as we sat at the dinner table, he broke down in tears with deep sobs confessing that he had lied to me. At first I didn't even remember to what he was referring. The confession provided an opportunity for rich biblical teaching, prayer, and renewal; it was a great blessing.

In Rick's uncertainty, he erred on the side of mercy by letting it go. He left it in the hands of God, and God did a work in his son's heart.

While we are limited in knowledge, God is not. He knows everything. Nothing is hidden from him. First Corinthians 4:5 tells us that "he will bring to light what is hidden in darkness and will expose the motives of the heart." Because of the great love God has for his children, we do not have to carry the burden of self-reliance in parenting. As much as we desire our children to walk in light, that desire pales in comparison to how much God desires them to. Therefore, we can pray with the certainty that God hears our prayers and acts in accordance with his great love and purpose.

TATTLING

David and Brad are playing cars in the family room. While David pushes his red Camaro with a T-top on the Hot Wheels track, Brad decides that throwing the cars at a target (i.e., Fluffy the cat) would be more fun. As Mom washes the dishes, off in the distance she hears the annoying and all too familiar words being yelled: "I'm telling Mom!" followed by, "Tattletale, Tattletale, I'm not playing with you anymore!"

Charging through the swinging door of the kitchen, the boys come to a screeching halt in front of Mom. David directs a smirk toward his fuming brother, then proceeds to present his case before the maternal judge.

UNDERSTAND THE HEART OF THE MATTER

Tattling is typically motivated by one sibling taking pleasure in the other sibling's suffering, which ultimately creates an atmosphere of opposition and conflict. Siblings who are committed to getting one another in trouble will wedge a thorn of distrust in their relationship, disrupting the harmony of the whole family.

Tattling reigns as one of the most common behavior problems among siblings. Unfortunately, in many homes it is overlooked rather than dealt with properly. Parents often pardon rather than correct the tattling child simply because they do not know how to deal with the issue. While some parents are frustrated with their inability to control the problem, others try to rationalize their decision to avoid correction.

"After all," reasons one parent, "if my child is doing something that he shouldn't, why does it matter how I find out?"

Another parent says, "If one of my children has been wronged by his sibling, I would rather he come tell me than fight back." While this sort of reasoning can seem right, it fails to get to the heart of the matter concerning the tattler.

Several quick-fix solutions often struggle for primacy in the parent's mind. For example, in the story about David and Brad, should Mom thank David for informing her of his brother's wrongdoing and punish Brad for throwing the car? Should she instruct both boys to put away the cars and play with something else? Should she separate them until they forget about the whole issue? While these seem to be reasonable next steps that don't involve correcting the tattler, they are not biblical, and they overlook the damaging effects tattling has on sibling relationships.

A wise mother will base her child-training decisions on God's Word. She will look past the outward behavior of the tattler and concern herself with the issues of the heart, teaching the child what the Bible says about delighting in the suffering of others. Through the power and strength of her Lord, Mom will uproot the weeds of foolishness, plant seeds of righteousness, and show her child how desperately dependent on God he needs to be.

Ask Heart-Probing Questions

When you're taking on tattling, be sure to ask questions that will cause the tattler to take his focus off what his sibling has done wrong and turn it onto his own sinful motivation. You might ask, "David, could it be that you are taking pleasure in getting your brother in trouble?" Have David think through the result he wants when he informs you of his brother's wrongdoing. Ask, "What are you hoping will happen to your brother as a result of your tattling?" Encourage him to ponder and verbally express what is in his heart. By teaching the tattler to determine his own motives, you are teaching him how to think through his actions and to recognize his own sinfulness. At this point, you are ready to point him to his need for Christ.

Reprove Your Child for Tattling

It is important that you show the tattler precisely what he is doing wrong according to God's Word. You might say, "Honey, did you know that one of the seven things that God hates is when someone causes trouble with his brothers?" (Prov. 6:19).

Confirm what the Bible says in Proverbs 17:5, "Whoever gloats over disaster will not go unpunished." You might say, "Sweetheart, if you are trying to get your brother in trouble for your own enjoyment, then you will get in trouble." In our home, the tattler faces the same consequences as the other child.

Train Your Child to Encourage

It is not enough to rebuke your child for tattling; you must also teach him how to depend on the regenerating power of the Holy Spirit to replace sinful behavior with God-honoring behavior. It is important for him to understand that he is sinful, but it is equally important, if not more important, for him to understand the righteous life he is free to live in Christ.

You might say, "David, Hebrews 10:24 says that we are to 'spur one another on toward love and good deeds.' If you ask God, he will help you to be an encouragement to others. Rather than tattling, what could you have said to encourage your brother?" If this is a new concept for the child, you may have to offer suggestions such as, "Mom says we shouldn't throw things in the house. I don't want you to get in trouble, so you better stop." After giving him an example, allow him to think of his own encouraging words.

The training will stick better if you require your child to practice the biblical alternative to his sinful behavior. Children tend to learn best in hands-on situations. Role-playing is an extremely effective way for the tattler to put God's Word into practice. Scripture commands us, "Do not merely listen to the word, and so deceive yourselves. Do what it says" (James 1:22). Role-playing trains the child to become a doer rather than just a hearer of the Word of God, equipping him to respond biblically to similar situations in the future.

Be sure to explain how we are all sinners in need of God's grace and help. Acknowledge that apart from God's power that enables us, we can do no good. Encourage him to pray for God's help to live in his righteousness.

Lead both children back to the scene of the crime, which, in the case of our story, is the family room. Allow Brad to throw (or, for the sake of Fluffy, pretend to throw) his car. Tell David to encourage his brother, in a gentle, self-controlled voice, to stop throwing. Require Brad to respond to David's rebuke by refraining from throwing the car and thanking his brother for his encouragement.

Children learn by repetition. Be willing to work with your children each time an opportunity presents itself. On those tiresome days, when you become weary from taking the time to train them, remember Galatians 6:9, "Let us not become weary in doing good, for at the proper time we will reap a harvest if we do not give up."

To Tell or Not to Tell

Not all tattling is wrong. In fact, there are times when it's necessary. It all boils down to motive. First let's examine wrong motives. There is tattling simply for the purpose of tattling, as in our story of Brad and David, but there is also tattling that comes when you've been sinned against. Even as adults, there is a great temptation to tattle when someone has sinned against us. When an injustice is done to us personally, we desire justification and approval for feeling hurt or angry. The quickest way to receive justification and approval is by presenting details to someone else and soaking in his or her reaction. It makes us feel better for someone to validate our feelings and come to our defense. Children are the same. If one sibling selfishly snatches a toy away from the other, the child who has been sinned against wants approval for feeling anger or hurt. He wants to be recognized as the victim, and he wants justice to be served. So he tattles.

THERE IS A DISCERNABLE DIFFERENCE BETWEEN A CHILD WHO IS TATTLING BECAUSE HE TAKES PLEASURE IN HIS SIBLING GETTING INTO TROUBLE AND A CHILD WHO IS INFORMING OUT OF LOVE.

"If your brother or sister sins, go and point out their fault, just between the two of you" (Matt. 18:15). This verse teaches that tattling is wrong. We are to teach our children to follow biblical instruction and pursue peace first by confronting the sinning sibling in private, keeping the matter between the two of them. If one sibling has gently rebuked the other, however, and the other does not adhere to the rebuke, the wronged sibling needs a means of escape for him to not become exasperated or angry. This, too, is biblical, as Matthew goes on to explain that if the sinning person refuses to listen, it is then appropriate to bring in someone else (vv. 15–16). To communicate this biblical instruction to your children, you might say, "Sweetheart, you may only come to me if you have confronted your brother first and he will not listen to you."

Another situation that may, at first, seem to be tattling but really isn't is when your child is genuinely concerned. Tattling out of concern for the well-being of another reflects a caring heart for others, which is a good, God-pleasing motive. There is a discernable difference between a child who is tattling because he takes pleasure in his sibling getting into trouble and a child who is informing out of love. The attitude in which the information is presented typically reveals motive.

There are occasions when a child should come directly to a parent: when another child is not heeding his rebuke and encouragement, when another child is endangering himself or someone else, or when another child is destroying property. If there seems to be confusion about how to know what kind of situation your child is in, take time to explain the difference between tattling and genuine concern. Discuss occasions when he does need to come directly to you, perhaps giving scenarios to help him with clarity. This way, when the time comes, your children won't feel paralyzed and unsure when something does require your immediate attention.

Cultivate Unity in Their Friendship

At the end of the day, it's important to deal with tattling because it affects the relationships between siblings. Take the time to remind your children that they will more than likely have a longer relationship with each other than anyone else they know. They will be friends long before they meet their marriage partners and usually long after their parents are gone. Encourage them to nurture their friendship and to seek every opportunity to develop a bond of closeness by always considering the feelings of the other.

You might ask, "Honey, how do you think your brother feels when you tattle? Will tattling bring you closer to your brother or tear you apart? How do you think it makes him feel when you encourage your brother rather than tattling?" Pointing his thoughts in this direction helps encourage him to be others-focused, rather than self-focused, which is, ultimately, the way to become more like Christ.

There were times I handled tattling well and times I handled it not so well, and I clearly recall the positive or negative effects my responses had on my children's relationship. When I merely accepted the tattling at face value and turned my attention to disciplining the child being told on, the one who was disciplined showed resentment toward the one who told, which affected their relationship in a negative way. However, when I questioned the motive of the one tattling, explained the damaging effects it has on their relationship, and guided him to go back and encourage his sibling with love and concern, I witnessed it unify their bond in powerful ways.

Explain how tale-bearing divides friends and how we are encouraged as children of God to "be kind and compassionate to one another, forgiving each other, just as in Christ God forgave [us]" (Eph. 4:32). This helps children understand the specific ways God has called them to treat one another. Also, according to Proverbs 19:11, we are blessed when we overlook someone's offensive behavior toward us: "A person's wisdom yields patience; it is to one's glory to overlook an offense." Directing our children's attention to God's will for their friendship helps them to see past one another's wrongdoings and develop an attitude of unity in their relationship.

Defying

Mom is folding clothes in her bedroom, while five-year-old Jenny is happily playing with her favorite doll, Tabitha, in the living room. Jenny's dad, who is away on a business trip, calls to check in. After Mom and Dad chat for a while, Dad is eager to hear the voice of his little princess.

Carefully setting up for a tea party, Jenny has just finished adorning her small pink play table with a lavender lace tablecloth. She has strategically placed the plastic teakettle and dainty matching tea cups and saucers for the ultimate tea-time experience. After politely pulling out the chair for her porcelain guest, Tabitha, and scooting her closer to the table, Jenny settles into her own chair, giggling with excitement. Just as she lifts her cup to take the first sip of the delicious pretend tea, she hears her mom call, "Jenny, I need you to come in here, please."

Not wishing to be interrupted, Jenny chooses to ignore Mom's instruction.

"Jenny, did you hear me? I said I need you to come in here," Mom calls out a little louder from her bedroom as she continues folding clothes.

Silence.

"Jenny! I know you can hear me! If you don't obey me right now, you're not going to be allowed to play with Tabitha for the rest of the day!"

More silence.

Fuming, Mom stomps into the living room. Handing the phone to Jenny, Mom spews, "Dad wants to talk to you. Why does everything have to be a battle with you? Why can't you just do what I say?"

Understand the Heart of the Matter

As parents who deeply love our children, we would like to believe their defiance results from circumstances beyond their control, rather than their hearts. Protective maternal instinct drives us to defend the goodness of our children and place blame elsewhere. Therefore, we often make excuses for their defiance. We deem them the victims rather than addressing the sin issue of the heart, which in this case is disobedience to our authority, ultimately stemming from selfishness.

"Tommy can't help it. He has trouble listening and doing what I say when he's busy playing."

"Poor Becky. She always gets cranky when she's tired or hungry."

"Oh no, Johnny must have woken up on the wrong side of the bed this morning."

Unfortunately, this sort of parenting teaches children to blame-shift rather than take responsibility for their own sin of disobedience. Children disobey not because they are busy, tired, hungry, or having a bad-hair day. They disobey because they are sinners who are selfish by nature. At the heart of disobedience is selfishness; it is desiring the advancement of one's own interests, wants, happiness, and satisfaction to the point of disobeying authority. Because children are born with a pull toward selfishness, which leads to defiance, they must be taught to live contrary to their natural desire to please themselves above all else and instead to dwell in harmony with God's plan for children to obey their parents and, ultimately, the Lord.

The sooner we help our children accept the reality of their depravity, the sooner they will recognize their need for Christ. Let us not delay pointing them to the redeeming power of our Savior by refusing to address their sin nature of disobedience. We must not be shocked by their disobedience or become frustrated and weary in our responsibility to train them. Rather, we must view every act of defiance as a precious opportunity to teach them about the atoning work of Christ.

Ask Heart-Probing Questions

When your child ignores or verbally defies your instruction, take time to stop what you are doing and address it intentionally, kneeling and making eye-to-eye contact. This ensures that you have her full attention. You might say something such as, "Jenny, I instructed you to come to me. Did you obey or disobey?" After waiting for her to verbally acknowledge that she disobeyed, you might ask, "Sweetheart, how did you disobey?" Requiring Jenny to identify exactly how she disobeyed helps her to take ownership of the sin in her heart, which, in turn, helps her to recognize her need for Christ.

Reprove Your Child for Disobeying

One command of Scripture is "Children, obey your parents in the Lord, for this is right. 'Honor your father and mother'—which is the first commandment with a promise—'so that it may go well with you and that you may enjoy long life on the earth'" (Eph. 6:1–3). In light of this scripture, as you proceed to reprove your child, you might explain, "Jenny, when you disobey me, you are disobeying God, and it will not go well with you. God put you in our care, and obedience keeps you safe. Sweetheart, I love you too much to allow you to disobey."

Train Your Child to Obey

As you move on to training, you might say, "Jenny, God's Word encourages, 'Children, obey your parents in everything, for this pleases the Lord'" (Col. 3:20). Be sure that your child understands that true obedience is complete, instant, and joyful. Teach your children that biblical obedience means obeying all the way, right away, and with a joyful heart.

I remember someone sharing this tool with me as a new mom. I found it helpful for instilling the meaning of obedience into the hearts of my children even before they were old enough to verbally communicate. I would ask, "Honey, how does God want you to obey?" After answering the question for them over and over, once they could communicate, they learned to answer, "All the way, right away, and with a joyful heart." This gave them a clear understanding as to what complete obedience looks like, as well as exactly what I expected from them.

As we talked about earlier, it is most effective to have your children physically put the training into practice. In our current example, once Jenny accepts that she has responded sinfully and understands how she should have responded, you might say, "Let's practice obeying all the way, right away, and with a joyful heart." Then you could recreate the scenario by having Jenny play with Tabitha again while you go back into your bedroom and call for her. When she immediately comes to you, be sure to offer a lot of praise. "Jesus is so happy when you obey Mommy (or Daddy)!"

Avoid Power Struggles

What if Jenny doesn't respond to your questions and is unwilling to role-play? What if her heart does not soften? Only God can truly change our children's hearts; a wise parent will strategically avoid power struggles. If Jenny does not answer a question such as "How did you disobey?" rather than creating an entirely new battle by demanding that she answer, simply answer for her. Answering for her does not compromise the fact that you are still feeding her the Word of God, which penetrates the heart (Heb. 4:12). If Jenny is unwilling to role-play, you might have her spend some time in her room alone, giving her time to reflect and calm down. Sometimes a cooling-off period can be beneficial toward attitude adjustment.

It is wise to avoid power struggles. Pray and ask God to help you recognize and avoid them. A common morning prayer for me when my children were young was *Lord, help me to be wiser than they are today!* Often, there are simple solutions to avoiding power struggles.

I recall a period of time during which I would become frustrated when I would call my children to dinner. While my children were growing up, it was our routine for them to watch television while I prepared dinner. With the table set and dinner hot and ready, I would call them repeatedly to come to the table, only to hear "Just a minute, Mom," which was typically followed by the same response several minutes later. After giving it more thought, I realized I was exasperating my children as much as they were exasperating me. If I were heavily engrossed in a television program that was abruptly interrupted without warning, I would be frustrated too.

GOOD PARENTING IS NOT SHOWN IN BEING A MILITANT DICTATOR BUT IN DEMONSTRATING RESPECT FOR OUR CHILDREN WHILE, AT THE SAME TIME, REQUIRING OBEDIENCE.

A simple solution that eliminated exasperation and demonstrated respect for my children came in the form of administering a five-minute warning. I would inform them, "Dinner will be ready in about five minutes, so y'all (we live in Alabama) need to find a place to pause your show." This worked well to mentally prepare them for change when they were engrossed in playing, homework, or anything else. Good parenting is not shown in being a militant dictator but in demonstrating respect for our children while, at the same time, requiring obedience.

MANIPULATING

Thomas is outside jumping on the trampoline with a neighbor-hood friend. Mom walks onto the back deck and instructs Thomas to tell his friend good-bye and come inside for dinner and homework.

With a disgruntled face, Thomas replies, "But I don't want to come in. I want to stay and play with Jimmy. Why do I have to come in now?"

Mom retorts, "I told you. Dinner is almost ready, and you need to shower and finish your homework. Stop arguing, put on your shoes, and come inside."

Thomas continues to jump. "I don't ever get to play with Jimmy. You never let me have any fun!"

UNDERSTAND THE HEART OF THE MATTER

When a child attempts to evoke an emotional reaction rather than a mature response from Mom or Dad to gain control of a situation, he is practicing manipulation. In an effort to achieve a specific desired outcome, the child uses manipulative words to influence or alter his parent's decision. Statements such as "You don't love me anymore" and "You never let me" are just a couple of examples of phrases crafted to instigate an emotional reaction for the child to get what he wants.

Younger children may cry, whine, beg, or throw temper tantrums to attain whatever it is they want. When they do this, they are *acting foolishly*. When Mom rewards the child's sinful attempt for personal gain by giving him what he wants, she is *responding foolishly*.

Older children may accuse, criticize, pout, ask *why* questions that are more about gaining control than about a genuine sense of curiosity, give you the cold shoulder, or withhold affection to manipulate your response. When they do this, they are *acting foolishly*. Mom may reward the child's sinful attempt for personal gain by defending herself, justifying her actions, blame-shifting, answering the *why* questions, or arguing. When Mom does this, she is *responding foolishly*.

God gave parents instructions for how to respond to manipulation in Proverbs 26:4–5: "Do not answer a fool according to his folly, or you will also be like him. Answer a fool as his folly deserves, that he not be wise in his own eyes" (NASB). This is not to say that children are "fools" but that they are capable of acting foolishly and in accordance with their sinful nature. When this happens, we need to recognize it, choose not to allow ourselves to be manipulated, and respond wisely.

The Bible gives us many examples of people, both friends and enemies, who tried to manipulate Jesus. Jesus never answered a foolish question or accusation with a foolish response. Instead, he responded in such a way that the person was never allowed to walk away from the conversation believing that he was "wise in his own eyes." Many times, Jesus showed the person his own foolishness by causing him to evaluate his own heart.

For example, Luke 10 recounts the time when Jesus came into the home of Mary and Martha. Mary sat at the Lord's feet and listened to his words, while Martha was distracted by all the preparations that had to be made for the guests. What Martha wanted was assistance in helping with the preparations, but rather than simply asking for help, she tried to manipulate Jesus into making Mary help.

Martha whined, "Lord, don't you care that my sister has left me to do the work by myself? Tell her to help me!" (v. 40).

JESUS NEVER ANSWERED A FOOLISH QUESTION OR ACCUSATION WITH A FOOLISH RESPONSE.

Jesus responded in such a way that Martha had to take her focus off what Mary was doing and onto the motives of her own heart. Jesus said, "Martha, Martha . . . you are worried and upset about many things, but few things are needed—or indeed only one. Mary has chosen what is better, and it will not be taken away from her" (vv. 41–42).

At other times, Jesus thwarted the manipulators' intentions by avoiding their questions altogether, thus demonstrating their foolishness to the crowd. For example, in Matthew 21:23–28, the chief priests and elders questioned Jesus' authority, hoping to undermine his ministry in front of the crowd. Instead of defending himself and inciting the controversy they sought, Jesus posed a question that exposed their own enslavement to popular opinion:

"John's baptism—where did it come from? Was it from heaven, or of human origin?" (v. 25). In other words, "Was John's ministry from the authority of God or done in John's own efforts?" The source of John's baptism—the Father, the Son, and the Holy Spirit—was the same source that gave Jesus his authority. Knowing the crowds favored John, the chief priests and elders didn't want to upset them by answering. When they refused to answer the question, Jesus responded, "Neither will I tell you by what authority I am doing these things" (v. 27).

Our responsibility in the face of foolishness and manipulation is to respond the same way Jesus did: putting the focus back on the motives of the heart. As parents, we can judge the words and actions of our children, but we do not have the ability to judge their thoughts and motives. If we are wise, however, we can help our kids evaluate what is in their own hearts and guide them in pulling out the foolishness that is bound up there.

Ask Heart-Probing Questions

One way Jesus exposed the true motives of those bent on manipulation was by asking heart-probing questions. Jesus often responded to a question or attack with another question to turn the accuser's attention away from trying to manipulate and onto his own heart and motives. Rather than responding to our children *in accordance with their folly* and demonstrating our own foolishness, we can wisely respond *as their folly deserves* and dissuade them from becoming wise in their own eyes.

You might ask, "Thomas, could it be that you are trying to make me feel guilty so that you can get what you want?"

Reprove Your Child for Manipulating

Avoid responding in accordance with your child's folly by not answering his manipulative questions. A foolish response to Thomas's charge that you never let him have fun might be something along the lines of "That's not true! I let you play with Jimmy three days ago. You get to have a lot of fun." Surrendering to his manipulative tactics by rewarding his sinful behavior would be even more foolish: "Well, okay. I guess you can play for another thirty minutes."

Instead of an emotional or guilt-based reaction, answer your child as his folly deserves by pointing him to Scripture. "Sweetheart, you should desire to honor and obey your parents more than you desire to play outside with Jimmy. Son, be careful not to become a lover of pleasure more than you are a lover of God" (Prov. 21:17; 2 Tim. 3:4).

Train Your Child to Weigh His Words

Once your child has obeyed, perhaps even later that evening, talk with him about avoiding the snare of manipulating rather than obeying. Help him understand the possible motives behind manipulative comments, questions, and accusations and how they keep him from obeying God by obeying your instructions. Remind him that Colossians 3:20 says, "Children, obey your parents in everything, for this pleases the Lord."

You might also take the opportunity to talk about how manipulation is typically an attempt to satisfy personal pleasure. While God delights in providing us with many things to enjoy, such as playing with friends, and wants us to take pleasure in his provisions, he also warns of the dangers of loving pleasure more than loving him.

Encourage your child to think before he speaks in similar future situations and to consider whether his motives are self-seeking or God-honoring before he responds. Explain that thinking through his responses before speaking is advised in Proverbs 15:28: "The heart of the righteous weighs its answers, but the mouth of the wicked gushes evil." A good question for him to ask himself before responding is "Am I obeying and loving God or trying to get my own way?"

Avoid Embarrassing Your Child in Front of Others

When possible, it is better to train your child in private rather than embarrassing him in front of others. Our goal is not to embarrass or humiliate our children but to train them up in the ways of the Lord. When we correct our children in front of others, we take their focus off the sin in their hearts and onto the embarrassment we have unnecessarily caused them.

Teachable moments are more effective when humiliation is not involved. When possible, take your child aside and issue the correction and training in private, as your child will be more attentive and teachable when not distracted by embarrassment.

Sometimes, it may be unavoidable to rebuke your child in the presence of others. If you find yourself in a situation where you are unable to remove your child to a private place for correction, you might simply lean down and quietly speak into his ear so that the rebuke and instruction are just between the two of you.

DISCERNING THE WHY QUESTION

There are two kinds of *why* questions: one that deserves an answer as it is posed out of genuine curiosity, and one that is a manipulative attempt to gain control. It is typically not hard to distinguish between the two. If you announce that your child needs to leave with you to pick up Daddy from work, when he typically arrives home in his own car, and your child asks why, it is likely he is honestly asking for an explanation. If you offer a solid explanation, and he whines, "Why?" in an attempt to stay home, that is a different story.

If your daughter is having a great time playing with her dolls in her room and whines, "Why?" after you have clearly explained it is time to straighten her room and get ready for bed, she is more than likely posing the question as a manipulative stall tactic to avoid straightening her room and going to bed. You have a choice. You can answer in accordance with her folly and cater to her stalling tactic by responding, "You have already been playing for an hour, and I already told you why." Or, you can answer as her folly deserves and help her to evaluate her own motives by asking a question such as, "Honey, could it be that you are more interested in playing with your dolls than pleasing the Lord? God says 'Children, obey your parents in everything, for this pleases the Lord'" (Col. 3:20).

TAKE EVERY OPPORTUNITY TO POINT YOUR CHILD TO CHRIST

In every teachable moment, always remind your child that he cannot master sin on his own. To drive it home, it helps to share age-appropriate examples from your own life where you fail to walk in righteousness and to express your gratitude for the forgiveness, atonement, and grace of God. Children tend to be more open about their own struggles when we are willing to humbly open up about ours.

I recall sharing my struggle with manipulation with my son when he was around five years old. First, let me explain something about my personality. I don't like change, especially change that involves my environment. I've lived in the same house for twenty-four years, and the placement of all the furniture in every room has never changed. Some furniture has been replaced, but it covers the same areas of floor as the furniture before. Once I determine how I think something looks best, I never feel the need to revisit it.

Not so with my son. The boy loves change. From around five years old, he would rearrange his bedroom. I remember him pushing his blue, car-shaped toddler bed to the other side of the room and moving his toy box to a different wall every other week. If he could move it, it was often moved.

Unlike Wesley, I thought his room looked best a certain way, so that's the way I wanted it to stay. I could have made furniture placement an issue of obedience, but because it was his bedroom, I wanted to give him the freedom to make a few decisions on his own about it. So, what did I do? I tried to manipulate the freedom I'd given him.

I would say things like, "It looks okay like this, but don't you think it looks better the way it was?"

He would respond with something like, "I think I like it to be different sometimes."

I would try again, reemphasizing the word *better*, and say, "Yeah, but don't you think it looks *better* the other way?"

After several attempts to convince him the room looked better the way I liked it, conviction washed over me when he finally nailed it as only a five-year-old can do sometimes. "Mom, I think you want me to think how you think, and I just don't."

Boom.

In that moment I recognized exactly what I was doing. I was trying to manipulate his thoughts and opinions. I confessed to him that I sometimes struggle with allowing people the freedom to have a different opinion from mine and explained in very simple terms how manipulation was one of the many areas of my life where God was still working. Wesley was quite forgiving of his mom's confession and was kind enough to point out my struggle many more times as he was growing up. Accountability is a good thing.

When we personally testify to our own weaknesses and our own need for God's intervention, it exemplifies how he is working in our lives and encourages our children that he can do work in theirs.

Wesley is grown and out on his own now, but he comes home for visits often enough that I've left his room as he last decorated and arranged it, which was during his young-twenties "hippie" phase. Yes—beads, tapestries, vinyl record player, John Lennon—the whole thing. Lord, help me.

INTERRUPTING

Desiring some much-needed adult conversation one day, Mom decides to invite a friend and her daughter over for lunch. Since her friend's daughter and her own daughter are the same age, Mom is hopeful the girls will entertain themselves so the adults can spend the afternoon chatting.

No such luck. The interruptions begin even during the initial phone call.

"Peggy, this is Linda. I was calling to see if . . . oh, hold on a second. Sweetheart, Mommy is on the phone. Please don't interrupt. Sorry, Peggy, we are still trying to teach Maddie to stop interrupting. Anyway, I was calling to see if . . . Maddie! I just told you to stop interrupting! Go watch your show until Mommy is off the phone. Okay, Peggy, I'm back. Anyway, I was hoping you and Brooklyn could come over for lunch. The girls could play and . . . Maddie! I am trying to talk on the phone, and you are being extremely rude! Peggy, let me call you back."

After giving full vent to her pent-up frustration, Mom calls Peggy back to extend the invitation while Maddie sits sobbing in her room. But when Peggy and Brooklyn come over for lunch, Maddie continues to interrupt the adults throughout the meal. Exasperated, Mom exiles the girls to Maddie's bedroom, hoping they will play contentedly and allow the moms to chat in the living room without interruptions. Maddie constantly runs into the living room, however, seemingly oblivious to the moms' conversation, and begins talking. Both moms spend the afternoon frustrated as they can barely complete a sentence without Maddie interrupting. Maddie spends the afternoon upset that her mom is angry with her and exasperated that she has things to say but receives a verbal lashing whenever she tries. Everyone loses out on what should have been an enjoyable afternoon.

Understand the Heart of the Matter

Due to a natural bent toward selfishness and pride, children automatically place a higher priority on themselves than on others. As a result, they deem what they want to say as being more important than respecting the conversations of others. When they want to express what is on their minds, they feel a sense of urgency, which leads to impatience, which leads to interrupting. It all boils down to selfishly placing their wants and needs above the wants and needs of others.

Ask Heart-Probing Questions

Constant interruptions while trying to have a conversation can be extremely irritating, making the temptation to speak harshly very real. As you work to reach your child's heart, be sure to apply Galatians 6:1: "Brothers and sisters, if someone is caught in a sin, you who live by the Spirit should restore that person *gently*. But watch yourselves, or you also may be tempted" (emphasis added).

Avoid lashing out with attacks such as, "I can't believe you are being so inconsiderate! I told you not to interrupt me while I am on the phone. You are acting so ugly!" Instead, help your child recognize the selfishness of interrupting by asking, "Honey, do you think it is kind or rude to interrupt me while I am talking to someone? Are you thinking about others or yourself when you interrupt?"

Reprove Your Child for Interrupting

As you move on to biblical correction, you might begin with wisdom from 1 Corinthians 13:4. "Sweetheart, the Bible explains that love is patient and kind. Love is not rude." Then you might move on to reference Philippians 2:3, and say, "God instructs us not to do things that are selfish. Instead, we are to consider the needs and feelings of others as being more important than our own. When Mom is talking to someone, how can you be more considerate?"

TRAIN YOUR CHILD TO BE CONSIDERATE

It would be exasperating to our children if we continually told them to never interrupt without providing a means of escape. We do not want them to feel as though their thoughts are unimportant. Rather than dismissively waving them away when we are engrossed in a conversation, we need to let them know we care about and value what they have to say. One effective way to teach your child to be considerate while you are engaged in another conversation is to require your child to place her hand on your arm (or wherever) whenever she has something to say.

You might begin with, "Maddie, I always want to hear what you have to say, but it is important that you learn to be respectful and considerate, rather than rudely interrupting." Then explain the new plan, and practice it until she understands how it works. Tell her that when she places her hand on you, it is the same as saying, "Mom, I have something to say, but I don't want to be rude by interrupting." When she does this, immediately place your hand on top of hers in acknowledgment. Explain to her that when this happens, it means, "Okay, I know you want to say something, and I will stop and allow you to speak as soon as I can."

Avoid making her wait too long. Find the first natural pause in the conversation, and then allow your child to speak. Be attentive as soon as you can so as not to discourage her, keeping in mind that younger children have shorter memories and attention spans.

Teaching children to place a hand on you rather than interrupting is not a biblical mandate. It is simply a tool to help prevent exasperation while you teach them to be kind and considerate, which *is* a biblical mandate.

"Excuse Me" (Not the Magic Words)

Many parents teach children to simply preface their interruptions with "excuse me." In my opinion, this isn't any less rude. Interrupting is interrupting, regardless of the preface. "Excuse me" is not the trump card that makes interrupting acceptable.

I had a friend whose child chanted this phrase constantly, and I found it just as rude and irritating. Someone could be in the middle of a sentence, and "excuse me" was all the child had to say to get Mom to unapologetically cut off the person speaking and give full attention to her child. It was as if the entire universe should realign and revolve around her child simply because she spoke the words "excuse me."

"Excuse me" is acceptable for "Excuse me, the kid down the street just set our cat on fire," but it is not acceptable for "Excuse me, I'd like everyone to immediately stop talking and pay attention to me because I am the center of the universe."

Siblings Interrupting Siblings (and Friends)

While children may learn to respect adults by not interrupting, sometimes they do not recognize the need to respect their siblings and peers with the same courtesy. If one sibling is quieter or less assertive by nature, it is likely that the more outgoing sibling will struggle with interrupting. Be alert and intervene when necessary in these situations by saying something such as, "Sweetheart, your sister was talking. Do you think it is kind or selfish for you to interrupt? You need to be respectful by listening and waiting until she finishes before you speak."

When all four of our children are home, the conversations can be lively and competitive, especially when we are all gathered around the table sharing a meal. We have three teenagers and one young adult. Two of our three teenagers are heavily involved in theatre. With theatre comes drama. With drama comes talkative, animated, assertive teens, whose voices are several decibels louder than the others'. They typically dominate the conversation.

Our youngest is quiet and speaks more softly. We have to mediate the conversation by waiting for the talkative two to take a breath and quickly grabbing the opportunity to ask the quieter one questions. When one of the chatterboxes chimes in before he finishes, we say something along the lines of, "Honey, Jackson was talking. You need to wait until he is finished, and then you can talk. Jackson, you were telling us about the bike race—?"

Teach more talkative children to divide and respect airtime with their siblings and friends. It may take a lot of practice and intervention on your part, but be patient. The more they practice being sensitive to other people talking, the more quickly they will learn to respond with respect, patience, and kindness.

What Example Are You Setting?

Children learn by watching and observing. Do they witness you monopolizing conversations with others? Some adults who hog airtime might argue, "I'm just not a good listener" or, "I have a hard time focusing when others are talking" or, "I'm just keeping the conversation going." Parents who monopolize conversations, however, are exemplifying the sin of pride. This sort of pride says, "I believe what I have to say is more important or more worthy of being heard. I am always right, I have all the answers, and I do not have time to listen to your insignificant thoughts."

Do your children witness you finishing sentences for your spouse or others, cutting them off before they are done, or becoming frustrated or impatient while waiting for them to finish a thought? These poor communication habits also exemplify pride. This pride says, "I am smarter and pick up on things faster. Therefore, I shouldn't have to wait for you to sort through this in your slow-thinking mind."

THE MORE YOUR CHILDREN PRACTICE BEING SENSITIVE TO OTHER PEOPLE TALKING, THE MORE QUICKLY THEY WILL LEARN TO RESPOND WITH RESPECT, PATIENCE, AND KINDNESS.

While it is important to not model pride while communicating with others, it is also important that we do not monopolize conversations with our children, finish their sentences, cut them off, or show frustration or impatience while they are talking. Be considerate when your child is talking, just as you expect them to be considerate when you are talking.

Avoid exasperating them by being on the phone all the time or placing calls and texts as your highest priority. If you and your child are having a conversation over lunch and the phone rings or a text comes in, wait until you have finished talking with your child before checking your phone and responding. This not only serves as a strong example of respecting others, but also sends a powerful message that what your child has to say is important to you.

It is tempting, especially for stay-at-home moms in need of adult conversation, to chat on the phone or text a lot. Believe me, I get it. But we need to be sensitive to how our children may perceive this. If you do have to answer a call, it can also speak volumes to your child if she hears you respond, "Peggy, let me call you back in a little while. Maddie and I are having lunch together and talking." What a blessing for your child to know she is loved, respected, and important to you!

Your Child's Need for Attention

When children constantly interrupt, it can be frustrating and make you want to tune out, but it's important to be mindful that your children do need your attention to a healthy extent. In fact, children who are often ignored tend to be more demanding and more prone to interrupting. It is certainly appropriate and biblical for your children to learn to put others' needs above their own, but it is also important that you model that same teaching by acknowledging and serving your children's needs.

Your children need time with you. Be sure to set aside time each day to take interest and listen, even if their topics of conversation seem silly. Because of their age or level of maturity, what may be deemed as unimportant to you can be very important to them, so it's helpful to engage in conversational topics of their choice while keeping in mind that they are still growing in maturity and communication skills. This can be exhausting at times, but resist the temptation of allowing your mind to wander. Listen intently and show interest in their thoughts and opinions by asking related questions.

When I was around five years old, I remember standing on the seat beside my daddy while he drove his pickup truck (this was around 1973, before child-safety seats and wearing seatbelts were required by law). With one arm wrapped around my daddy's neck, I would point from one thing to the next as the scenery zoomed by and ask, "Daddy, what's that? Daddy, what's that? Daddy, what's that?"

Like any good daddy, he patiently answered, until finally he was worn out with responding to my endless questions. He paused, shook his head, sighed deeply, and stated, "Sugar, I don't know."

Shocked by his unexpected response, I removed my arm from around his neck, cupped his chin to turn his eyes toward mine, grinned widely, and replied with great confidence, "Oh, Daddy! You know everything!"

I don't recall him ever avoiding a single silly question after that day. I was blessed with a faithful, patient, loving daddy—a daddy who was delighted that his daughter thought he knew everything.

Fast-forward eleven years. My parents were suffering a discouraging time of teenage rebellion when I turned sixteen. Daddy would encourage other parents by telling the story of that day in his pickup truck with the moral of the story being "Listen to and talk with your children while they are still young and believe you know everything, because one day, when they turn sixteen, they may look at you and yell, 'Oh, Daddy! You don't know anything!'"

Some of the most precious conversations I have had with my children when they were younger, and even when they were older, were at bedtime. I made it a habit to lie in bed with them individually and just listen to whatever they wanted to talk about. I avoided bedtime being a time to correct and rebuke. Instead, we treasured our nights of sometimes lighthearted laughter and sometimes deep conversations. If you have several children, you might consider having designated nights for each one. When you set aside time just for them, they feel loved, valued, and important. When you meet your children's needs by spending quality time alone with them, their hearts are more attentive and receptive to your teaching.

Complaining

It is that time of year again. The seasons are changing, and with Andrew's annual growth spurt, his clothes from last year are bursting at the seams. It is time to make that agonizing shopping trip for new clothes: the one that typically results in a battle of wills, a disgruntled attitude, and an annoying twitch in Mom's left eye. How Mom dreads even mentioning that four-letter word (s-h-o-p) to her little man! The torture of listening to his complaining makes it a gut-wrenching fiasco every year.

Mustering up her most cheerful voice, Mom sticks her head in Andrew's room. "Andrew, it's time to get up, honey. Rise and shine! We need to get some clothes shopping done before we go to the baseball game this afternoon."

Andrew pulls the sheet over his head and growls, "Mom, you know I hate shopping! It's boring, and I get tired of trying on everything."

"Well, sweetheart, I know you don't like shopping, but sometimes we just have to do things we don't enjoy," Mom chirps.

"But Mom, it always takes so long, and it's Saturday. All the stores will be packed. I don't like waiting in those long lines."

"Andrew, you don't have a choice," Mom explains with a *here we go again* sigh. "We can't go during the week because of school and homework. We have to go on a Saturday."

"But Mom!" Andrew complains. "I have to get up early for school all week and church on Sundays. Saturday is my only day to sleep in and not be in a hurry. I never get to just relax in the mornings. I hate getting up early, I hate shopping, and I hate trying on itchy new clothes!"

Understand the Heart of the Matter

Some may say that complaining is an issue of personality, having to do with whether you are positive or negative, whether you see the glass half full or half empty. However, complaining is not a personality problem. It is a heart problem. Regardless of personality type, our tendency to complain typically derives from how we view and feel about a person or situation. Complainers tend to base perspectives on feelings. If something causes us to feel bad, we complain. But feelings should not be the barometer that measures response. Rather than allowing our feelings or moods to dictate our perspective, we need to focus on which lens we will view the situation through—the temporal or the eternal. The temporal is controlled by feelings. The eternal is controlled by faith in Christ and a deep-rooted trust in his promises.

Through the eternal lens we are reminded that "in all things [good and bad] God works for the good of those who love him, who have been called according to his purpose" (Rom. 8:28).

God desires us to get beyond the way a situation looks or feels and live in the hope that he is in control of all things. In believing this, we can "give thanks in all circumstances; for this is God's will for [us] in Christ Jesus" (1 Thess. 5:18). When we view every situation through the lens of the gospel, we see God's goodness.

God is good all the time, no matter what kind of day we are having, what kind of mood we are in, or what unpleasant circumstances we are facing. When we dwell on God's goodness in every situation, even the ones that seem unfair or undesirable, it changes the way we view those situations and the way we handle them. And out of hearts of thankfulness, we complain less and less.

Solomon encouraged us not to search for the bad but to seek out the good. He also indicated that there are consequences for both: "Whoever seeks good finds favor, but evil comes to one who searches for it" (Prov. 11:27). As sanctified children of God, we are empowered by the Holy Spirit to take captive critical thoughts that cause us to complain, to edify others through speaking encouragement, and to live thankfully in God's goodness. In living through the empowerment of Christ, complaining is replaced with thankfulness.

Ask Heart-Probing Questions

As we approach a child who complains, rather than dreading the complaining and mentally preparing ourselves to endure it, we can choose to view the situation through an eternal lens. Look at it as a valuable occasion to insert scriptures into the child's heart, teaching him why complaining is wrong and how God can help him to live in the joy of thankfulness.

When he voices his complaint, you might say something like, "Honey, is your attitude showing thankfulness and contentment? Do you think the things you are saying will make this shopping trip pleasant or miserable? Is there joy in your heart when you are complaining?"

Reprove Your Child for Complaining

As you prepare to correct his behavior, you might say, "Your attitude is not showing respect for me, nor is it pleasing to God. The Bible says, 'Do everything without grumbling or arguing'" (Phil. 2:14). Remind him that his attitude is a choice: "Sweetheart, with God's help, you can choose to have a good attitude even when you don't feel like it. God says we are to 'take captive every thought to make it obedient to Christ' (2 Cor. 10:5). He also says we are to speak words that will benefit those who listen (Eph. 4:29), and your complaining is certainly not benefiting me."

If you are thinking, *In fact, your complaining is about to completely tick me off,* you may want to leave that part out.

Train Your Child to Be Thankful

As you move on to training, consider reminding your child, "It is God's will that you be thankful and joyful in all circumstances (1 Thess. 5:16–18). Rather than complaining, what can you be thankful for in this situation?"

If he presses his lips together, folds his arms, and cannot think of a single thing, you might prompt him with a grin, saying, "Perhaps you could be thankful that God has provided income to purchase clothes so that you do not have to go to school naked." There is always something for which to be thankful.

As a part of ongoing training, whenever he starts to complain, have him stop and consider something for which he can be thankful. Require him to verbally replace each complaint with a statement of thankfulness, even if it is as simple as being grateful for a sunny day, an umbrella, a nice lunch with Mom, or an air-conditioned car.

TEACH BY EXAMPLE

Complaining is a heart issue we see a lot of in our children, but we should also consider our own attitudes. When you sit down at the dinner table, do you tend to complain about everything that went wrong during the day rather than pondering and voicing thankfulness? I will confess that I tend to complain and look at the negative in situations. I have also observed that once I allow one negative comment to come out, it starts a snowball effect. The whole "taking captive every thought" goes out the window, and I begin to spout every negative thought that pops into my head. I have been told that I can get quite ridiculous with it.

One practice that has helped me deal with my own heart is to begin each day praising God and thanking him for even the little things, such as a hot shower, a cool breeze, great conversation with family around the dinner table the night before, and so on. Throughout the day, when something I could complain about pops into my head, I ask God to help me see how I can be thankful instead. I do not always get it right, but even when I don't, I am thankful for the forgiveness and grace of God that covers me when I blow it.

In fact, I did it just now. Here I was writing about how to help your children regarding complaining, and my laptop just completely spazzed out on me. While I was typing, my curser jumped to a different paragraph. In scrolling down to get back to the right place, I completely lost track of the point I was trying to make. And what did I do? I loudly blurted, "This stupid piece-of-junk laptop!" Then I stopped and asked God to help me take my thoughts captive before I got on a warpath of complaining. I refocused and thanked God that I do not have to suffer the inconveniences of handwriting or using a typewriter but rather I have the luxury of owning a laptop—even if it *is* a piece of junk.

Because it is God's will that we be thankful and joyful in all circumstances, it helps to be constantly looking for opportunities to praise God for all things, especially when we are tempted to do the opposite. We can voice little prayers of thankfulness throughout the day. When I am tired of being in the kitchen cooking, a quick prayer of thankfulness for a fully equipped kitchen and a husband and children for whom to prepare meals causes my attitude to transform into one that is pleasing to God. Also, as I rely on the empowerment of Christ to view cooking through the eternal lens of serving God and my family rather than through the temporal lens of obligation that leads to complaining, my heart follows and is filled with joy.

Talk with your children about your own struggles with complaining. Be open with them about the times you have chosen to complain rather than to show thankfulness and about the spiritual state it put you in. Also share the times God helped change your ungrateful attitude to a heart of gratitude. Discuss the differences. Children are more receptive to gospel teaching when you are willing to be open and honest about your own struggles and need for Jesus.

Teach Biblical Examples

The Bible is full of people who exemplified gratefulness and faith when it might have been tempting to complain. When our children are struggling with contentment, we can point them to the godly men and women of Scripture who handled their difficulties in a Christlike way.

Joseph was a man whose life reflected the example of Christ, though he lived many centuries earlier. After suffering unjust treatment from his brothers, rather than complaining, Joseph exhibited his faith in God through the words he said to them: "You intended to harm me, but God intended it for good" (Gen. 50:20). Joseph trusted that God was in control, even in the worst of situations. Therefore, he praised God rather than complaining about the hardships he had suffered because of his brothers.

Teaching our children about men such as Joseph is a great way to help them understand how complaining reflects a distrust in God's plan and his ability to bring good from all things. The testimony of others helps them relate truth to real-life situations where complaining could hinder perspective. Through the personal examples of others, they learn that when we are willing to trust God even in the worst of situations, the tendency to complain melts away, and we begin to respond as Jesus responded to his upcoming encounter with evil in the Garden of Gethsemane: "Shall I not drink the cup the Father has given me?" (John 18:11). The cup the *Father* has given me. Facing death by crucifixion would certainly qualify as the worst of situations. Certainly worse than a shopping trip for clothes. Yet Jesus did not whine, "Why me?" He did not complain about the evil being unjustly brought against him. He knew the Father's plan served a much higher purpose than his temporal situation.

When things are not going their way and circumstances are not ideal, children, like us, are naturally tempted to complain. We can encourage them by redirecting their perspective. Circumstances seem less important when their minds are turned toward God's active involvement in their lives, his sovereignty, and, ultimately, his eternal plan and reward. The temptation to fret and grumble over discomfort or trouble is more likely to disappear in light of the truth spoken to us in Romans through the apostle Paul: "I consider that our present sufferings are not worth comparing with the glory that will be revealed in us" (8:18).

Another man we can tell our children about is Paul, who set a great example in being thankful, rather than complaining. When he and Silas were preaching the gospel in Philippi, they were dragged away, beaten, and bound in stocks in the inner cell of the jail. Yet every time Paul remembered the Philippians, he did not complain but voiced thankfulness. Paul had been in a horrific situation in Philippi. He suffered beatings and insults (1 Thess. 2:2), yet he continued to speak words of encouragement and thankfulness. How was Paul thankful after such devastating hard times? He *chose* to be.

It is important for children to understand that the way they respond to difficult or unpleasant situations is a choice, and few examples in Scripture reflect this empowering truth as clearly as Paul. He chose not to ponder aspects of his situation that would lead to the temptation of complaining. Instead, he set his mind and heart on things above. He determined to live out of the mercies and grace of God toward his adversaries despite his horrific circumstances. He resolved to dwell on the love he had for Jesus and the love Jesus had for him. Therefore, he could live out of the hope of the gospel. That's the same hope we want to live out and teach our children to live out as well.

Take some time to explain to your kids that if they choose to search for the bad in people and situations and compulsively voice negativity, they will live in the joyless bondage of ungrateful hearts. But when they choose to look to the intervening work of Christ, he enables them to overcome ungrateful, complaining hearts.

Of course, the greatest example we can point our children to is Jesus. Hebrews 4:15 confirms that when he was here on earth, Jesus was tempted in all the same ways we are tempted: "For we do not have a high priest who is unable to empathize with our weaknesses, but we have one who has been tempted in every way, just as we are—yet he did not sin." We cannot say that Jesus did not complain because he did not face the same situations as we do. Jesus encountered every situation, yet he did not sin. Therefore, he also encountered the temptation to complain, but he never did.

Jesus always exemplified what it means to trust the Father in all things. Through the indwelling power of the Holy Spirit, God enables his children to do the same. May we teach our children not to focus on the negative, which leads to complaining, but to take captive every thought, making it obedient to Christ and expressing an attitude of gratitude through praising God in all situations.

My Daughter the Fork

With shoulders slumped and a downcast look, my daughter Alex plopped down on the couch, crushed that she wasn't cast as the lead role of Belle in *Beauty and the Beast*. She was thirteen, and her life was over (always a flair for the dramatic).

> May we teach our children not to focus on the negative, which leads to complaining, but to take captive every thought, making it obedient to Christ and expressing an attitude of gratitude through praising God in all situations.

"Alex, honey, it's not the end of the world. There will be other plays," I encouraged.

"Right, but I'm a fork in the 'Be Our Guest' ensemble. I mean, couldn't I at least have gotten Babette the feather duster or Chip the teacup? I'm nothing more than flatware, Mom!"

After the first few rehearsals, Alex came home complaining. She complained about having to be there for the whole rehearsal when she was only in one small part of the show. She complained about people who she thought were poorly cast. She complained about the choices the directors were making and people showing up late for rehearsal. On and on and on, she complained over every little thing. I knew that all her complaining really boiled down to not getting the part she wanted. She didn't want to be a behind-the-scenes character. She wanted to be front and center stage.

Wanting to reach the heart issue behind her complaining and encourage her with Scripture, we talked about Luke 16:10: "Whoever can be trusted with very little can also be trusted with much, and whoever is dishonest with very little will also be dishonest with much." To help her understand how this truth might apply to her situation, I said, "God honors our faithfulness with little things by entrusting us with bigger things. So I believe if you'll be a faithful fork, one day you'll be a beautiful Belle."

Because there is power when we personally testify to how God's truth has played out in our lives, I then took it a step further and shared a part of my own journey with Alex. Alex was familiar with my ministry of speaking and writing, but I'd never told her how it had all come about, how the truth of this verse had become real to me in a personal way. So I seized the opportunity.

My ministry had originally begun with leading a small group of twenty or thirty moms where I, along with a few others, took turns teaching on the high calling of motherhood. This led to creating the *Wise Words for Moms* chart I mentioned earlier, which was basically a practical application of the biblical principles I had learned from my favorite parenting book, *Shepherding a Child's Heart* by Tedd Tripp.

I found an address for Tedd Tripp and mailed him a copy of the finished product with a thank-you note, explaining how his work had inspired the content. I didn't expect to receive a response, except maybe something along the lines of an auto-graphed postcard with Tedd's picture. Imagine my surprise when I received a call from his son who runs Shepherd Press, the publisher of *Shepherding a Child's Heart*. I remember his words like it was yesterday: "Ginger, this is Aaron Tripp at Shepherd Press. We would like to publish *Wise Words for Moms*." Drop the phone. Gulp. Resuscitate.

Just before the chart went to print, I had an idea. At our moms' group, my presentations were recorded on cassette tapes (yes, I am that old) for the moms who missed the meetings. I requested that Shepherd Press list the topics on which I had spoken along with my landline phone number (yes, I am that old) in the hopes that moms might like to purchase tapes of my presentations for encouragement. I grinned from ear to ear as I made five copies of each presentation on my little double-cassette recorder, stacked them neatly on the table by the telephone, and waited for it to ring.

You know the verse that says God will do immeasurably more than all we ask or imagine? Well, he did. Rather than moms calling to order tapes, event planners from churches and homeschool conventions began to call, requesting that I come speak. And so my national speaking ministry was launched.

Fast-forward three years. I had been speaking at parenting conferences and homeschool conventions all over the country and was entertaining the idea of adapting the material into a book. Tedd Tripp was scheduled to keynote at a homeschool convention in Montgomery, Alabama, which was not far from where I lived. Tedd Tripp: my hero, my mentor, the one and only, the parenting guru of all time. The. Tedd. Tripp. He was going to be fifty miles from my hometown. With shaking hands and a quivering voice, I called his son Aaron at Shepherd Press and requested to meet with Tedd over lunch while he was in

Alabama. Aaron said he would pass on the message but couldn't make any promises.

During the weeks leading up to the convention, I waited with anticipation, jumping every time the phone rang, but I never heard from Tedd. No response at all. Not even an autographed postcard. I lost all hope of a face-to-face meeting, which was totally embarrassing, as I had told everyone north of the equator that I might be having lunch with Tedd Tripp. Then, the morning Tedd was scheduled to keynote, my phone rang. The voice on the other end said, "Hi, this is Tedd Tripp. I am available to meet with you today for lunch if that's still an option."

My first thought was that it must be a prank from one of my friends, Tim, who knew how worked up I'd been over the possibility. I rolled my eyes and came very close to saying, "Whatever, Tim" and hanging up the phone. I'm so glad I didn't, because after a few exchanges, I realized it really was Tedd Tripp. Drop the phone. Gulp. Resuscitate. We arranged to meet that afternoon.

As Tedd sat across the table from me, eating a cheeseburger and fries, I presented my idea for compiling my presentation outline into a parenting book. Determined for him to hear every word of my well-rehearsed speech, which I had practiced all the way to Montgomery, I talked nonstop the entire time he ate. Finally, I paused and took a breath. That's when the moment I'd been waiting for took a turn for the worse.

He slowly slid the outline for my book back across the table and said, "It's a good idea, but I think you're too young to write a parenting book. Contact me again in ten years."

You don't know me, but suffice it to say I don't easily take no for an answer, especially when it is something I am passionate about. Someone once told me I could sell a Bible to the Devil if I set my mind to it. With my heart hammering in my chest, I lifted my chin, raised my right eyebrow like Scarlett O'Hara, slid the outline back across the table, and, with all the courage I could muster, replied, "I'm thirty-three, which is around the same age Jesus began his ministry, and remember what Paul told Timothy in 1 Timothy 4:12 about teaching the things of God? He told him not to be intimidated because of his age."

To my relief, a huge grin stretched across Tedd's face. He picked up my outline, stuck it in his bag, thanked me for lunch, and told me he would look it over. Two years later, *Don't Make Me Count to Three!* was released, expanding a national ministry into an international ministry.

Never in a million years would I have thought that faithfulness in leading a small group of moms would lead to an international ministry. Faithfulness in the little things leads to trust with bigger things. I've confessed many of my failures in this book, but this time I finally get to tell you about one of the few things I got right. As I explained to Alex, when I first began in ministry encouraging a group of twenty or thirty moms, it would have been easy for me to find things to complain about. I could have grumbled over how much time it took me to prepare the messages for the meetings where only a handful of moms showed up. I could have complained about having to bring snacks and drinks when others didn't volunteer. I could have complained if no one acknowledged the work I put into it or if no one expressed thankfulness in how the fruit of my labor was used in their life.

There were many things I could have chosen to complain about. And I must confess, I am prone to complaining. But this was one time when I got it right. I chose not to complain but to be thankful for the small opportunity God gave me at each meeting to bring encouragement to moms. And God blessed the choice I made.

Alex ended up being the happiest little fork to ever grace the stage of a *Beauty and the Beast* production. And years later, she would reap the rewards of her faithfulness in performing many more fork-type roles without complaining, by landing several Belle-type roles, just as her mama had testified.

BLAME-SHIFTING

Matt steps off the school bus with a bad attitude. With shoulders slumped, backpack dragging behind him, and his homework reflecting a big red F tightly clutched in his hand, Matt walks into the house, slams the door, and goes straight to his room without speaking to anyone. When his sister Jessica enters his room a few minutes later, she and Matt begin to argue so loudly that Mom must intervene.

"What's going on in here?" Mom questions.

"I told Jess to get out of my room because I have to study, and she got mad at me and won't leave!" yells Matt.

"Well, sweetheart, it sounds as though you weren't very nice about explaining your need to study to your sister," Mom states as she sees angry tears welling in Jessica's eyes.

Matt glances at his sister, tightens his face, and blurts, "I got an F on my homework assignment, because Jess insisted on watching a movie last night that lasted two hours rather than watching the short sitcom I wanted to watch, so I didn't get to finish my homework."

"Are you saying it is your sister's fault you got an F on your homework assignment?" Mom asks.

Realizing his sister might not pass as the most convincing scapegoat, Matt adds, "Well, her and my stupid teacher who doesn't know how to explain anything. I mean, no one in the class likes her, Mom. She is a terrible teacher, and no one understands her. It really doesn't matter how much time I spend on homework when my teacher doesn't know how to teach."

UNDERSTAND THE HEART OF THE MATTER

I must confess that my husband and I are professional blame-shifters ourselves. It started about a year after we got married. You see, his compulsive need to place blame elsewhere rubbed off on me and caused me to become a blame-shifter too. Of course, he would say the opposite. All right, in all fairness, let's just put it this way: if there were two blame-shifting teams that needed worthy captains, Ronnie and I would be your best candidates for the jobs. Unfortunately, our hypocrisy has caused problems when we correct our children for blaming others rather than taking responsibility for their own actions. They look at us like, *Really? Are you seriously going to launch into a sermon on blaming others when you two would go to your grave arguing over who left the garage door up last night?* And the gavel falls.

Blame-shifting is a way of escaping the responsibility of our own actions by projecting blame onto someone else. When we switch the focus from ourselves by pointing a finger, we do not have to admit our failings or deal with fault. At the heart of this calculated detour is a prideful unwillingness to confess that we are imperfect sinners, which is dangerous territory for God's children.

When we engage in blame-shifting, we dismiss personal guilt and shun the very purpose of the cross. If we are unwilling to admit sin, then we imply that the crucifixion was a fool's errand.

> WHEN WE ENGAGE IN BLAME-SHIFTING, WE DISMISS PERSONAL GUILT AND SHUN THE VERY PURPOSE OF THE CROSS.

Along those same lines, when we do admit sin but make excuses for it, we act as though circumstances bring validity or justification for sin. This sort of blame-shifting expresses a soft view of sin, which produces a cheap view of grace.

Conversely, when we admit and confess sin, trusting in Christ for atonement, we can live in a deep appreciation for his grace. In taking responsibility for sin, we no longer have to own it. Christ bought and paid for all sin so that his children do not have to carry the burden of it anymore. And that is good news for me, for you, and for our children.

In understanding and applying what we learn about the heart of the matter, we must check our own hearts and responses, as well as call our children to do the same. We need to humble ourselves and accept blame when we make a mistake. Not all mistakes are sinful. Accidentally leaving the garage door open at night is not sinful. The sinfulness comes in the prideful unwillingness to admit the capability of making a mistake. When I point my finger at my husband, I am saying, "I am better than you. If there is trouble of some sort, it must be your fault, because I am too good for it to be mine." We are commanded not to walk in vain conceit, however, but in humility, valuing others above ourselves (Phil. 2:3). To more effectively train our children, we must take the plank out of our own eyes before pointing at the speck in theirs (Matt. 7:3).

Jesus explained, "Whoever has been forgiven little loves little" (Luke 7:47). If we want our children to truly love and worship God for all he has done and walk in the freedom he offers in Christ, then we must help our children grasp the weight of their sin. They cannot do that through blame-shifting. But if we instill in them a sense of personal accountability, they will understand and better appreciate God's sacrifice for them.

Ask Heart-Probing Questions

When you're dealing with a child who is blame-shifting rather than accepting responsibility for his choices, it helps to start by steering his thinking in the right direction. You might ask questions such as, "Could it be that you are trying to cover over your own sins by blaming your sister and your teacher?" To further help your child evaluate his own heart and take responsibility, you might add, "Without blaming someone else or making excuses, I want you to examine your own heart and tell me what you did."

Reprove Your Child for Blame-Shifting

Talk casually with love about how blame-shifting is a form of pride that hinders our relationship with God. Do so without falling into angry accusations. You might consider discussing wisdom from Proverbs: "Sweetheart, when you try to cover up your own wrongdoing by blaming someone else or making excuses, you will not prosper. I understand that you may be frustrated with your grade and perhaps even your teacher, but blaming and yelling at your sister and then criticizing your teacher is not beneficial for anyone. God knows what is in your heart and has mercy on those who confess sin. Proverbs 28:13 says, 'Whoever conceals their sins does not prosper, but the one who confesses and renounces them finds mercy.'"

Train Your Child to Admit and Confess Sins

As you continue the discussion and lead your child toward confession, you might explain, "Matt, while failing to complete a homework assignment is not necessarily sinful, it can become a dangerous cycle to always blame others rather than taking responsibility for our own choices and actions. When God's children get into a habit of not accepting responsibility for even the little things, it can easily lead to a temptation to hide sin, which hinders our relationship with God and the work he wants to do in our lives. Son, it is when we admit and confess sins that God works in our hearts. First John 1:9–10 says, 'If we confess our sins, he is faithful and just and will forgive us our sins and purify us from all unrighteousness. If we claim we have not sinned, we make him out to be a liar and his word is not in us.'"

As he starts to understand the deeper implications of his words, gently lead him to think and respond biblically. You might ask, "Honey, in light of what the Bible teaches, how could you have responded differently to this situation?" It is okay to coach our children in how they can put what they are learning into practice. You might suggest that rather than yelling at and blaming his sister he could have taken responsibility for his own actions by saying something along the lines of, "Jess, I got an F on my homework because I chose to stay up watching a movie with you last night. I really need to start working on my homework by seven tonight." You might also suggest that rather than complaining about his teacher not explaining things well, he could approach her after class or school and say something like, "I'm having a hard time understanding the lesson. Would you mind allowing me to explain what is confusing me so that you can help me see what I'm missing?"

Offer Biblical Examples

One of the most powerful ways to help children take ownership for their own blame-shifting and relate to potential consequences is to share personal examples from the lives of people in Scripture. Possibly the most well-known biblical example of blame-shifting happened after the fall of Adam and Eve, so that's a good place to start. God had commanded the first couple not to eat from the tree of the knowledge of good and evil. Both disobeyed God's command, but when God asked Adam, "Have you eaten from the tree that I commanded you not to eat from?" Adam blamed God for putting Eve in the garden with him. He also blamed Eve for giving him the fruit, saying, "The woman you put here with me— she gave me some fruit from the tree, and I ate it" (Gen. 3:11–12).

You might help your children visualize the story and possibly get a giggle out of them by asking something like, "Can you picture the couple ducking behind a banana tree and adjusting their fig-leaf britches as they heard God approaching?"

Just between us parents, what I can picture is the *uh-oh* expression on Adam's face after he threw Eve under the bus and then realized she would most likely have a strong opinion regarding his response. Eve probably turned to Adam and said, "Oh—my—gosh. You did *not* just say that." Uh-oh is right. No banana for Adam tonight.

While Adam took no responsibility for his own sinful choice and action, Eve was no different. When God asked, "What is this you have done?" Eve blamed the serpent, saying, "The serpent deceived me, and I ate" (v. 13). Personally, I would be tempted to note that Adam blame-shifted first, which influenced Eve to do the same, but I will admit that line of thinking could *possibly* come from my own compulsive need to blame-shift. I can only imagine the blame-shifting that might have taken place had Adam and Eve owned a garage.

The moral of the story that you want your children to take to heart is that while Adam and Eve tried to steer the blame elsewhere, they put nothing over on God. God knew the sin of their hearts. Blame-shifting did neither of them a bit of good and did not prevent any of the consequences. In fact, when they tried to hide from God out of their shame and fear, this put a strain on their relationship with him (vv. 8–10). The same is true for us. We want to help our children realize that no matter how hard they try, they cannot hide from God by refusing to take responsibility for sin. Repentance and restoration cannot occur without responsibility. God already knows anyway, so it is silly and pointless to try and hide.

Confessing and repenting is a hard discipline, but it is one we need not fear. Children need to understand this truth, and sharing biblical examples with them helps them understand. Through the life lessons of ourselves and others, we want to steer our children away from blame-shifting and motivate them toward confession and repentance. Once they begin living in this way, they begin to truly understand that where sin abounds, grace abounds all the more (Rom. 5:20).

Set the Right Example

The practice of taking responsibility and repenting is an important Christian discipline. Not only does it keep our hearts in check and the ongoing work of Christ active in our lives, but it also authenticates our Christian witness to our children. Our credibility as Christians springs not from the absence of fault, but from how we respond to it. When our children witness us sin, we diminish the power of our witness to some degree. When we humbly accept blame and demonstrate a heart that seeks Jesus for atonement, however, we increase the power of our witness. We are all sinners in need of God's mercy and grace. Rather than desperately seeking to preserve our reputations through a denial of fault, we must acknowledge our frailty and then point to the one who never fails.

Be Willing to Transfer Responsibility to Your Child

In teaching kids to accept responsibility for their own actions, rather than shifting blame elsewhere, you might also consider practical ways to help them develop a sense of personal responsibility for simple tasks. Requiring them to take responsibility for themselves in practical ways can serve as a stepping-stone to their accepting a higher level of personal responsibility in spiritual ways.

One of my most frustrating and ongoing challenges as a mom has been getting my kids out of bed in the mornings. The funny thing is I spent the first five years of their lives trying to keep them in bed. Once they became school-age, I couldn't get them out.

One of the cons for homeschooling is the issue of no accountability to be "at school" on time. Mom isn't quite as intimidating as a principal, and there is no sense of embarrassment from walking in twenty minutes late and interrupting class, resulting in twenty sets of eyes staring. Detention hall? What's that?

I recall one school year that started out no differently, with me announcing the wake-up time the night before, the kids agreeing to the wake-up time the night before, and the whole plan going out the window the next morning.

The first week of school involved me walking past my kids' bedroom doors every morning in ten-minute intervals with statements like, "You need to get up!" (I turn on the coffeepot). "Why are you not up?" (I check e-mail). "Are you still not up?" (I pour a cup of coffee). "I thought I told you to get up!" (I return a phone call). The next thing I knew, I was totally frustrated. Standing in the hall, draped in my oversized, white terrycloth robe, one hand on my hip and the other gripping my coffee mug, I blurted, "What is wrong with you people? It is *ten o'clock* in the morning!"

Finally, I realized I was not doing them any favors hounding them to get up. In addition to being annoying, I was hindering them from learning to be accountable and responsible. Rather than learning to wisely govern their own time, I had caused them to become dependent on me doing it for them.

I knew things had to change. I didn't want my children to be sluggards who turned on their beds as doors turn on hinges (Prov. 26:14), or lovers of sleep who grow up poor (20:13). And I didn't want to be the nagging, quarrelsome woman (27:15) whose family would rather live on the corner of a roof (25:24). Instead, I wanted to be the mom who spoke with wisdom and faithful instruction (31:26), whose children grew up working diligently for the Lord (Col. 3:23), and, of course, calling their mama blessed (Prov. 31:28).

The solution began with a trip to Walmart. I allowed both kids to pick out their own alarm clocks. We made the purchases (I even threw in a couple of packs of gum for good measure) and made our way home. After showing them how to set their alarms properly, I made a shocking announcement: "From now on, you may decide what time you get up in the mornings." Both jaws dropped. I continued, "Yes, you guys are old enough to get up on your own, without my nagging. Therefore, I will no longer tell you to get out of bed." Once it really sunk in that they had not misunderstood what I was saying, you would have thought it was Christmas morning.

I allowed the kids time to celebrate for a few minutes, soaking in all the hugs and kisses before adding, "With your new freedom, there also come a few responsibilities."

"Oh, anything, Mom!" they eagerly agreed.

"I expect both of you to be showered, have your rooms

clean, devotionals done, breakfast eaten, and working on school assignments by 9:00 a.m."

The deal was, they could get up whenever they wanted, as long as they fulfilled the requirements. They eagerly agreed.

What happened when they slept too long and didn't meet the requirements? They lost the freedom to watch a television show that night. Each morning, the choice was theirs. If they chose to be responsible, they got to enjoy the freedom to watch a show at night. If they chose not to be responsible, they lost that freedom. No nagging, just plain and simple choices.

The results? Morning tensions lifted. My children learned to govern their own time. They learned there were consequences for being irresponsible and rewards for being responsible. They learned the law of the harvest.

A couple of years ago, my husband and I faced this same challenge with his teenage boys, my stepsons, who were both attending public school. Mornings were rarely off to a good start with repeated instructions to get out of bed and cranky responses to our nagging. So, we decided to make a change. There would be no more nagging. We instructed them to set their own alarm clocks for whatever time they wanted. We made it clear we were willing to allow them to face the natural consequences of detention hall or even suspension to teach them to be responsible for themselves.

The results? Thankfully, they never had detention hall or suspension after we transferred the responsibility of time management over to them. They matured through learning to take responsibility for themselves, and mornings in the Hubbard home became much more peaceful.

Now we've come full circle with our teenagers and young adults. In the mornings, they get up on their own just fine, but they don't want to go to bed at night. It's a never-ending cycle, but it's a cycle that I know one day I'll miss.

TEASING

Vince and David are playing in Vince's tree house when suddenly they hear leaves crunching close by. They crack open the tree house door and peek out to see who the intruder is. It is Julie, Vince's younger sister. Decked out in her favorite princess costume, Julie is skipping toward the tree house while singing to her baby doll securely cradled in her arms.

"Oh no," complains Vince. "She probably wants to play in the tree house." Vince would rather hang out with David alone, but he remembers his parents talking to him about being kinder to his sister.

Julie climbs the ladder and walks in on the boys. "Hey, what are you guys doing?" she chirps as she straightens the oversized tiara on her head.

"We're hanging out and watching the squirrel traps through the spy holes," David replies. "We caught one last week and almost got bit when we let him go. You wanna watch with us?"

Excited over the invitation, Julie grins and eagerly nods,

which causes the tiara to fall over her eyes. "Yeah, that sounds cool!" she says, rushing to the nearest spy hole while adjusting her tiara again.

At first the three of them get along well, but then Vince begins teasing—something he has started doing often, especially when his friends are around.

"So, which princess are you supposed to be today, Julie? Stephanie the Stupid or Delores the Dumb?" Vince laughs as he glances at David to gauge his friend's reaction. Vince is pleased as David chuckles. Mission accomplished.

Mom approaches the tree house with three popsicles just in time to hear Julie's response.

"You can make fun of me if you want, but I am actually Snow White, which means all the squirrels like me, so if you are nice to me, I might help you catch one!" Julie is determined to fight back, but the tears begin pooling in her eyes.

"Oh yeah, I forgot how all the forest animals were like Snow White's pets," retorts Vince. "I'm sure if we wait around long enough, all the squirrels and birds will show up to curl your hair and tie your bows. Don't you think so, David?"

Julie swallows the swelling lump in her throat, but it's no use. The tears begin to trickle down her cheeks.

Understand the Heart of the Matter

Teasing can manifest in many ways, such as mocking (imitating someone to make him appear and feel stupid, silly, or ridiculous) or insulting (verbally ridiculing or belittling someone to make him appear and feel inadequate or less significant). Whether the teaser is criticizing, belittling, or making fun in a joking way, biblically, teasing falls under the category of "unwholesome talk" that fails to benefit the listener. In fact, unwholesome talk does just the opposite. It tears down the listener, which is a direct violation of God's commands to love others (John 13:34) and build them up (Eph. 4:29).

There are at least three motives for teasing: to get attention, to entertain, and to verbalize what you truly mean, with the latter typically losing the merit of truth when "Just kidding" is quickly added after the so-called teasing remark. All three motives are selfish in nature, as they bring the teaser a form of satisfaction at the expense of hurting someone else. If there is an audience, as in the case with Vince, David, and Julie, the motive is most likely geared toward receiving attention and entertaining. It is more important to Vince to get David's attention by making him laugh than it is to preserve his sister's feelings. At the heart of Vince's motive is a selfish attempt to gain favor. Vince is putting his own need for attention over the needs of his sister, which violates God's command to value the interests of others over our own (Phil. 2:3–4).

While Vince's motive is to receive attention and entertain, other motives can be equally as wrong. For example, to use teasing to say what is really on one's heart is equally as selfish and hurtful. Some people use teasing or joking to send hidden messages because they lack the nerve to come right out and tell the other person how they really feel. When they are called on it, they backpedal with "I'm just teasing." The "I'm just teasing" is a falsehood, because, in fact, they spoke how they really felt. They were truly not teasing.

Others have difficulty expressing their true feelings simply because they don't have healthy communication skills, so they mask their true feelings by teasing and joking. Either way, this sort of teasing lacks the merit of truth, which is a matter clearly addressed in Ephesians 4:25: "Therefore each of you must put off falsehood and speak truthfully to your neighbor, for we are all members of one body."

No matter the reason or motive, using teasing to express feelings is not in line with God's instructions. To verbalize what is true in your heart and then follow it with "Just joking" is deceitful. In Proverbs 26:18–19 we are told, "Like a maniac shooting flaming arrows of death is one who deceives their neighbor and says, 'I was only joking!'" We are to say what we mean and mean what we say. We are to let our yes be yes and our no be no (Matt. 5:37). This verse also warns that "anything beyond this comes from the evil one."

Biblical and unselfish communication involves speaking truth in love and encompasses the motive to bring good, not harm. According to Ephesians 4:15, it is through this sort of communication that believ-

> BIBLICAL AND UNSELF-ISH COMMUNICATION INVOLVES SPEAKING TRUTH IN LOVE AND ENCOMPASSES THE MOTIVE TO BRING GOOD, NOT HARM.

ers grow in maturity in Christ: "Speaking the truth in love, we will grow to become in every respect the mature body of him who is the head, that is, Christ."

Ask Heart-Probing Questions

When you find your child teasing another, it's wise to start a conversation with him that first helps him view teasing from a biblical perspective. You might say, "Honey, in Philippians we are encouraged not to do things out of selfish ambition, but to value the needs of others above our own. Could it be that you are putting your need to entertain David above the feelings and needs of your sister? How would you feel if you were Julie? Julie's feelings were hurt to the point of tears. Did your words show love by building her up, or did they tear her down?"

Reprove Your Child for Teasing

As you transition into biblical reproof, you could use wisdom from Matthew 7:12 by saying, "Son, we are told in Matthew that we should treat others the way that we would want them to treat us. Would you want your sister to treat you the way that you have treated her? Honey, when you tease, you are using unwholesome talk that dishonors God and hurts your sister. The first part of Ephesians 4:29 warns, 'Do not let any unwholesome talk come out of your mouth.'"

Train Your Child to Edify Others

Now that you've set the scriptural basis to avoid teasing, follow up with training in how to be an encouragement instead of a discouragement. You might say, "Not only are we commanded to not allow unwholesome talk to come out of our mouths, but the second part of Ephesians 4:29 tells us to speak 'only what is helpful for building others up according to their needs, that it may benefit those who listen.' Your words did not benefit your sister;

they hurt her. The good news, however, is that when God gives us commands, he also enables us through his Spirit to follow those commands. I encourage you to pray and ask God to help you only speak words that will benefit and build up your sister."

Building Up Versus Flattering

As we teach our children to edify others, they need to understand that encouragement is truthful words spoken for the purpose of spiritually benefiting others, not flattery, which is lies spoken for selfish gain. Flattery is insincere praise that is undeserved and is usually excessive. It is spoken not to improve or encourage, but to manipulate and gain an advantage. The flatterer uses lies to lure the recipient, causing him to fall victim to the flatterer's charms and desires for personal gain and control. The flatterer always has ulterior motives. Of these people, the Scriptures warn, "They follow their own evil desires; they boast about themselves and flatter others for their own advantage" (Jude 1:16) and, "They flatter with their lips but harbor deception in their hearts" (Ps. 12:2).

Flattery is the manipulator's tool powered by lies. We are told not to trust the flatterer: "Not a word from their mouth can be trusted; their heart is filled with malice. Their throat is an open grave; with their tongues they tell lies" (Ps. 5:9). The Scriptures speak strongly about those who seek their personal pleasures and interests above others: "For such people are not serving our Lord Christ, but their own appetites. By smooth talk and flattery they deceive the minds of naïve people" (Rom. 16:18).

Encouragement, on the other hand, is for building up and

should be spiritually beneficial to the recipient. Encouragement does not look for something in return, but is genuinely motived out of love, the best interests of others, and a wholehearted desire to strengthen their faith through spurring them on toward love and good deeds (Heb. 10:24). What we say must never be designed to cause others to be ingratiated to us, but to Christ. The words that come out of a Christian's mouth should be sincere, loving, and honest. They should be a response to the other person's true needs and assist in motivating them to know, serve, and praise God.

When we speak edifying words, we also help one another guard against sin's lure. The enemy, Satan, is constantly on the prowl. First Peter 5:8 tells us, "Your enemy the devil prowls around like a roaring lion looking for someone to devour." Christians are bombarded from every side with enticements to sin. Because the world is full of temptations to lure God's people away, it is every Christian's duty to edify and encourage one another constantly: "But encourage one another daily, as long as it is called 'Today,' so that none of you may be hardened by sin's deceitfulness" (Heb. 3:13).

We have a mutual need and responsibility to impart spiritual edification and encouragement to strengthen one another's faith as we wade through life's ongoing spiritual battles. In Romans 1:11–12, Paul wrote, "I long to see you so that I may impart to you some spiritual gift to make you strong—that is, that you and I may be mutually encouraged by each other's faith." Not only are we to talk about Scripture and edify our brothers and sisters in their Christian walk, but we are to teach our children to do the same.

Is It Ever Okay to Tease?

But what about "good-natured teasing"? That is, teasing without selfish motives or the intentions to hurt another. In my family, my dad is often the center of this type of "ribbing," as some call it. When we're all together, we love to reminisce and laugh about some of the funny things my dad has done. He can laugh at himself without taking offense, so it makes him an easy target.

There are many stories of my dad unintentionally bringing comedy into our lives, such as the first time my mom brought home a computer. Daddy picked up the mouse, aimed it at the computer, and proceeded to click as if it were a television remote control. Mama doubled over with laughter and coffee spewed from her nose while Daddy shrugged and asked "Whaaat?" We have not stopped talking and laughing about it since.

Then there was this past Easter lunch when Daddy was going through the buffet line at our house. We had a small, round Canz (Bluetooth wireless speaker) softly playing music on the counter beside the food. Daddy thought it was a saltshaker. I was close to deliria, laughing so hard that no sound was coming out, as I watched him first vigorously shake the Canz speaker over his mashed potatoes and then examine it with confusion when no salt came out, trying to figure out which end would work. My stomach muscles were sore for a week.

Another good story involved the time Daddy was doing minor repair work upstairs at our house. Never a good idea. Suddenly, we heard a loud *crash* at the bottom of the stairs, followed by a low moan. We rushed around the corner and found him crumpled in a heap, tangled with a stepladder and rubbing a knot on his forehead. Once we confirmed he was okay, he explained how it had happened. Rather than carrying the step-ladder under his arm horizontally, he thought he could carry it vertically down the stairs. Daddy is a fairly short man, so this made the ladder longer than his legs. He explained that he knew he was in trouble as soon as he took his first step down and the ladder touched the ground before his feet. It created a sort of pole-vault effect. The more we pictured it, the more we laughed. And laughed. And laughed. And told everyone. And laughed some more.

Okay, one more Daddy story, and then I'll move on. This was back when I was a teenager working with Daddy in his barbe-que restaurant. We were extremely busy with a line of customers all the way from the register counter to the front door entrance. Since Daddy is all about serving customers quickly, he ran (liter-ally) to the back stockroom to refill the large pickle bowl. When running back out (in front of all the customers), he slipped on a spot of grease, and both feet came out from under him. He landed completely flat on his back holding the pickle bowl upright on his chest. He didn't miss a beat. He jumped up and continued sprint-ing to the food preparation counter without losing a single pickle. It was like something straight out of a *Peanuts* rerun with Daddy starring as Charlie Brown. The story ended up all over town, spreading laughter throughout the community.

I could go on and on, but I think you get the idea about what kind of teasing Daddy receives. Seriously, the man should have his own reality show. Because Daddy finds his lack of technical ability and silly antics as humorous as we do, he laughs right along with us and takes delight when we share his stories with all who will listen.

Personally, I do not think this is the sort of teasing that God warns against. It all boils down to whether the teasing is rooted in selfishness or a motive to hurt, or in our God-given desire to simply enjoy humorous situations. In addition to motive or intent, however, we must also weigh the needs, emotional bents, personalities, and reactions of others, especially if the humor involves laughing at something someone else has done. It must be considered that some people are more sensitive than others, do not find humor in their actions, and take offense when others do. Because Daddy loves to laugh at himself and delights in others finding humor in his antics, our good-natured teasing is not sinful. If he did take offense or experience hurt, it would be sinful. It is never okay to seek entertainment at the expense of hurting someone else. When evaluating whether the situation is an instance of harmless ribbing or hurtful teasing, take a moment to consider the heart and intention behind the words being spoken.

Sin-Corrupted Humor

God designed us to bring him glory. Sometimes that manifests in us giving thanks, and sometimes it looks like us laughing and finding amusement, pleasure, delight, and enjoyment in him and his creation. Good-hearted laughter at and with others that does not bring harm or hurt is one way we enjoy the humor he has given us.

Unfortunately, like all good things God gives his children, there are times when sin corrupts and perverts humor (often by way of teasing) into a behavior that is not sanctioned by or pleasing to our holy God. God takes sinful teasing very seriously. When a gang of boys was teasing the prophet Elisha about his bald head in 2 Kings, he called down a curse on them in the name of the Lord. Two bears came out of the woods and mauled forty-two of them (2 Kings 2:23–24). Now that's a story that'll get your kids' attention. Elisha was the Lord's prophet. To ridicule Elisha was to ridicule the Lord. The severe consequences the boys in the story suffered because of teasing were God's warning to all who would scorn the Lord's prophet.

We can learn from the story of the boys who jeered at Elisha, "Get out of here, baldy!" God created Elisha's bald head, just as he created us all with different personalities, characteristics, appearances, and interests. To make fun of any aspect of the unique qualities of God's creation is to criticize the Creator himself. Proverbs 17:5 says, "Whoever mocks the poor shows contempt for their Maker." Therefore, Christians are not to tear one another down through hurtful teasing that dishonors God. Instead, we are to "encourage one another and build each other up" (1 Thess. 5:11).

AGGRAVATING

Gunnar and Amy are at each other's throats all day. Looking for ways to get a rise out of his sister, Gunnar is playing every card in the deck. Amy responds to Gunnar's antics with everything from crying and screaming to tattling and lying on her belly while kicking and pounding the floor. Mom is frazzled and frustrated.

"Gunnar, stop swinging Barbie by her hair and yelling for your sister to watch! You know that upsets her!"

"Gunnar, stop jabbing your sister with the lightsaber and making Darth Vader breathing noises! You know that scares her!"

"Gunnar, stop running in circles around your sister and making train sounds! Can't you see that your sister doesn't like that?"

"*Stop!*"

Gunnar's response is the same after each rebuke: "Okay, but I'm just playing with her."

Tired and frustrated, Mom tries forcing Gunnar to apologize. He half-heartedly mumbles an insincere "sorry" to get Mom off his back but starts obnoxiously mocking and repeating everything his sister says as soon as Mom is out of earshot. When Amy runs to tell, Mom separates them for an hour, instructing each sibling to spend time alone in his or her own bedroom. Once the hour is up and the children are allowed to play together again, the cycle of Gunnar obnoxiously aggravating and Amy negatively responding continues. Mom threatens to banish both children to their rooms for the rest of the day but knows she needs to come up with a better plan of action.

After brainstorming for a solution, Mom thinks she is on to something when she instructs Amy, "Honey, when Gunnar is aggravating you, just act like it doesn't bother you, and he'll stop."

Mom's advice works for a little while, but then Gunnar begins scheming. He grins as he decides to play his trump card with what he affectionately refers to as "The Lion Game." The game involves Gunnar getting down on all fours and growling as he chases Amy through the house—and it is a surefire, tried-and-true way to provoke his sister.

As usual, the Lion Game works like a charm and gets Amy riled up. She screams for Gunnar to stop as she runs through the house, leading the lion right to Mom's feet.

"*Mom!* Gunnar is being mean to me!" Amy cries in anger. "Please make him stop chasing and growling at me!"

Understand the Heart of the Matter

It's so easy to get caught up in addressing the outward behavior rather than the heart issue behind aggravating. When the outward behavior is the only thing addressed, however, the problem will continue to manifest itself in different forms. In other words, the child may obey your command to stop one method of aggravating, only to move on to another method equally as irritating.

The child who lacks the skill to evaluate what is in his own heart, his true motive behind aggravating another person, cannot discern the wrong in what he is doing. Because he lacks that skill, he doesn't understand the common denominator in each behavior; therefore, it continues to show up in various forms. It is the parent's responsibility to help children understand that taking delight in aggravating and provoking others is wrong. Children need to learn how to view aggravating from God's point of view and recognize the sin of taking joy in causing someone else to suffer. They need to know that the sin of stirring up conflict is so important that it is listed as one of the seven things God hates (Prov. 6:19).

Parents must realize we must do more than give our children the answer (which is to stop aggravating). We must teach them why that is the answer. Once they gain an understanding of their own sinfulness and repent, they are better equipped to govern their own behavior rather than the parent repeatedly offering the answer to no avail.

Ask Heart-Probing Questions

To help direct children to understand their motive behind aggravating, we need to observe the situation, then ask a few pointed questions that will cause them to evaluate their hearts. In the earlier situation, Mom might begin with something such as, "Gunnar, judging from your laughter, you seem to be having a great time growling and chasing your sister around the house. Are you having as much fun as you look like you're having?"

Allow him to answer as he cannot deny that he is enjoying himself. Then have him focus on his sister's feelings.

"Is Amy having as much fun as you are having?"

Allow him to answer as he cannot deny that Amy is not enjoying herself. Take it a step further by asking him to verbalize how Amy is responding (crying, screaming, tattling, etc.). Once it has been determined that Amy is suffering from Gunnar's aggravating, which has obviously served as ongoing motivation for Gunnar to continue, you might ask, "Honey, are you delighting in Amy's suffering?"

Reprove Your Child for Aggravating

Help focus your child's attention on what God says about stirring up trouble and delighting in someone's suffering. You might say, "Sweetheart, Proverbs 6:19 explains that one of the seven things God hates is when one of his children stirs up trouble with another. To delight in your sister's suffering is not showing love to her. In 1 Corinthians 13:6 we are told that 'love does not delight in evil.'"

Train Your Child to Pursue Peace

Explain to your child how God has called us to purpose in our hearts to promote peace rather than stir up trouble. You might tell him that God's Word instructs us to make every effort to do what leads to peace (Rom. 14:19), as God has called all his children to live in peace with everyone (Heb. 12:14).

The child who struggles with aggravating might also find it encouraging if you remind him that God gives joy to those who promote peace (Prov. 12:20). While there may be a temporal, flesh-tickling sort of fun in aggravating his sister, it is nothing compared to the rich and spiritually satisfying joy that God gives his children when they obey his commands by pursuing peace with others.

As you take the proactive step of training your child to pursue peace, take both children back to the scene of the crime—in this case, where the lion first began the attack. Amy was the victim here, but it is also a teachable moment for her as she did not rightly respond to her brother's attempts to provoke. You might encourage Amy that rather than screaming, crying, yelling, and tattling, she could have promoted peace by responding to her brother with self-control. It is okay to give Amy an example of what to say so that both children gain a better understanding of how to resolve conflict biblically. Have Amy say to her brother something along the lines of, "Gunnar, it makes me unhappy when you growl and chase me like a lion. Please stop doing that." Remind Gunnar that since God has called him to seek and pursue peace, he needs to respond in a way that pleases God. Coach him in a simple and appropriate response, such as, "Okay, Amy, I'll stop."

> THE MORE WE SOW BIBLICAL INSTRUCTION INTO OUR CHILDREN'S HEARTS NOW, THE MORE WE (AND THEY) WILL REAP THE PEACEFUL FRUIT OF BIBLICAL OBEDIENCE LATER.

Don't Give Up

Teaching our children scriptures and walking them through how to put those scriptures into practice is vital, but it can also be tiring. It is something that has to be done over and over, and it can take a lot of time and effort, making it hard to be consistent in implementing this kind of instruction. When my children were younger and struggled with aggravating each other daily, I had to walk them through this sort of training many, many times before I saw the fruit. But, once I saw the fruit of them learning to govern their own actions by learning to evaluate their own hearts and then responding biblically on their own, it was highly rewarding and well worth the efforts.

We must understand that training our children in these sorts of situations is not a one-time thing. And while the light at the end of the tunnel seems far away, this season of training will be gone before we know it. We need to make the most of it while it's still here. The more we sow biblical instruction into our children's hearts now, the more we (and they) will reap the peaceful fruit of biblical obedience later. As our children begin to look past their outward behavior and understand their own hearts, they will become better equipped to govern their own actions. This is our goal. We must not lose sight of it, and we must not lose heart on the days when it seems our efforts are in vain. I have included the following verse in a previous chapter, but it was one to which I tightly clung when I was raising my children, and it certainly warrants repeating: "Let us not become weary in doing good, for at the proper time we will reap a harvest if we do not give up" (Gal. 6:9). Hang in there. The harvest will come.

BRAGGING

"Mom," says twelve-year-old Keith over breakfast. "Did you see that second goal I scored last night? Coach Nickels said it was the best kick of the season. The crowd really went wild, didn't they?"

Mom walks over to the kitchen table and lays a napkin beside Keith's plate. "Yes, it was a great kick, but you'll need this napkin to wipe your face if you don't stop drooling over yourself."

Keith laughs and begins talking around the waffle in his mouth. "Yeah, yeah, I bet all the parents were talking about it too. What were they saying? Were they impressed? They had to be impressed. It was quite an impressive kick."

Mom pours orange juice into Keith's glass. "Yes, dear, they were all impressed. I think they were almost as impressed as you are with yourself! You need to finish breakfast so you're not late for school. I wouldn't want you to miss out on any compliments or back pats from your local fans," she says with a grin.

As Mom is driving Keith to school, he begins confiding in her about a girl in his science class. "Did I tell you Elaine Harper has a crush on me? She keeps staring at me during science. I also notice that she always walks close by me in the halls in between classes. My friend Eric told me that he overheard Elaine telling one of her friends that I was the smartest guy at our school. She's right, you know. I am one of the only guys in my grade in the honor society. Hank Stevenson is the only one with a GPA that is higher than mine, but I'm sure that will change because I am way smarter than him."

"Yes," Mom agrees. "You are a very smart young man, but you would be even smarter if you did not brag on yourself so much. Conceit is an ugly thing, Keith."

"Oh, Mom, why are you always trying to change me? I'm just stating the facts." Keith shrugs as he grabs his backpack and exits the car.

Understand the Heart of the Matter

Bragging on oneself is an expression of pride. While some argue that prideful bragging is birthed from a heart of genuine conceit and love of self, others argue that those who seek attention through bragging are actually insecure and do not think highly of themselves at all. As a cover for their deep insecurities and low self-esteem, they verbally elevate their qualities, talents, abilities, and successes above others'. They try to convince people they are something they are not. They shamelessly insert themselves into the spotlight in an attempt to make a name for themselves, while inside their hearts lurks a suffocating sense of self-loathing.

While this theory about the origins of prideful bragging is quite popular, I can find no evidence for it in God's Word. Even if the theory were true, however, the insecure person's efforts to make up for their own self-loathing would still be self-motivated and self-serving, coming out of, perhaps ironically, a love of self. Love of self is grounded in pride. Therefore, whether the act of bragging stems from genuine insecurities or genuine conceit, it is still fueled by a prideful desire to exalt oneself. It in no way is characterized by a love for others or a desire to glorify God, which is in direct opposition to Scripture: "As it is, you boast in your arrogant schemes. All such boasting is evil" (James 4:16).

God hates pride and arrogance of all kinds (Prov. 8:13), which includes bragging on oneself, rather than on Christ. We are told that God will not tolerate it in Psalm 101:5: "Whoever has haughty eyes and a proud heart, I will not tolerate." The Scriptures are also clear, giving numerous examples, that there are consequences for boasting. When the Pharisee elevated himself by favorably comparing himself with others, bragged about fasting twice a week and giving a tenth of all his riches, not only did God say he was not justified in his bragging, but he also added, "For all those who exalt themselves will be humbled" (Luke 18:14). Another example comes from Nebuchadnezzar's response to God giving him sovereignty and greatness and glory and splendor. When Nebuchadnezzar demonstrated pride and arrogance, he, too, suffered consequences: "But when his heart became arrogant and hardened with pride, he was deposed from his royal throne and stripped of his glory" (Dan. 5:20).

According to Matthew 6:2, we are not to toot our own horns to receive honor from others: "So when you give to the needy, do not announce it with trumpets, as the hypocrites do in the synagogues and on the streets, to be honored by others. Truly I tell you, they have received their reward in full." We are not to use our gifts, talents, and abilities to be seen by and impress others. Jesus said, "And when you pray, do not be like the hypocrites, for they love to pray standing in the synagogues and on the street corners to be seen by others. Truly I tell you, they have received their reward in full" (v. 5).

At the heart of bragging is a sinful tendency to put our trust in ourselves and our abilities rather than in God. We are warned against this in Proverbs: "Those who trust in themselves are fools, but those who walk in wisdom are kept safe" (28:26). Bragging demonstrates a false sense of self-sufficiency. It models a works-oriented faith in ourselves and is driven by our own efforts. However, our works "are like filthy rags" (Isa. 64:6), and our faith and redemption must rest in nothing more than the atoning work of Christ. "For it is by grace you have been saved, through faith—and this is not from yourselves, it is the gift of God—not by works, so that no one can boast" (Eph. 2:8–9).

> AT THE HEART OF BRAGGING IS A SINFUL TENDENCY TO PUT OUR TRUST IN OURSELVES AND OUR ABILITIES RATHER THAN IN GOD.

Ask Heart-Probing Questions

It is important for children to understand that we are created to bring glory to God and not ourselves. When we brag on ourselves, we are taking credit for something that does not belong to us. We are created by God, for God. All talents and abilities are given to us and are to be used for God's glory and honor, not our own. In order for Keith to evaluate the motive of his heart, you might ask questions along the lines of, "Sweetheart, do those words bring glory and honor to God or yourself?"

Reprove Your Child for Bragging

In reproving lovingly, humbly, and with complete dependence on God for heart-changing results, you might say, "Keith, we are warned in Scripture that God will not tolerate a proud heart (Ps. 101:5). God also warns of the consequences of a proud heart, one of them being, 'When pride comes, then comes disgrace' (Prov. 11:2). It does not bring glory to God when we speak with vain conceit. Not only are we commanded not to brag on ourselves, but according to Romans 12:3 we are not to even *think* of ourselves more highly than we should. Instead, we are to think of ourselves with sober judgment, which recognizes that the only good we have is from and for the God we serve."

Train Your Child to Walk in Humility

As your child learns to put off bragging, start training him to put on humility in its place. You might say, "As Christians, we are called to walk in humility and consider others better than ourselves (Phil. 2:3). It is to God's glory and our own good when we avoid bragging on ourselves and nurturing a conceited heart, as we are told that 'with humility comes wisdom'" (Prov. 11:2).

We can humbly accept the praise of others as long as we keep a right perspective on it, which involves an inward and outward redirecting of that praise to the God who deserves it. We are commanded in Proverbs 27:2 to "Let someone else praise you, and not your own mouth; an outsider, and not your own lips." In explaining this to Keith, you might say, "Honey, others do brag on you, and that is okay as long as you recognize that the abilities and talents you have are not your own, but attributes that God has given you to be used for his great glory."

Avoid Fueling the Flame of Conceit

To take it a step further, let's consider how we as parents can head off pride developing in our children before it comes out of their mouths. We can do this by being more careful about how we praise them. The Scriptures tell us that it can be beneficial to brag on other people. In Proverbs it clearly states that appropriate praise of others in relation to their service and devotion to God is something in which we should engage: "A woman who fears the LORD is to be praised" (31:30). We also know that Paul rightly boasted about the churches (2 Cor. 7:14) and that Jesus commended six of the seven churches that he spoke of in the book of Revelation.

Proper boasting and praise of other believers can be helpful and encouraging. However, it can also be a stumbling block to a child who struggles with bragging and conceit. We do not want to fuel a prideful heart, so we need to give careful consideration to the way we encourage our children. When acknowledging a talent, strength, or gift in a child, we should always give God the glory for blessing the child with that talent, strength, or gift. This instills a Christ-centered awareness in them through the years.

Asking questions that help them acknowledge God, the giver of all good things, will guide them in giving God the glory rather than seeking it for themselves. When they succeed or excel, you might ask, "How did God equip and enable you for this particular task? How did he go ahead of you, preparing and making provisions for you? How did he cause the details to work out?"

An others-oriented and Christlike mentality can also be instilled by encouraging them to consider and thank others who God has brought into their lives to offer help and influence. If Keith's dad or a family friend or a coach spent time teaching Keith how to kick, thanking that person can steer Keith away from bragging and conceit. If Keith struggled with a particular subject in school and someone took the time to explain and help bring understanding, thanking that person might help Keith acknowledge the work of Christ in his life.

We do want to encourage our children to let the light of their God-given talents and strengths shine brightly so that others can see the good works God has done. It is even more important, however, that we encourage them to give God the attention and glory rather than calling attention and glory to themselves. "In the same way, let your light shine before others, that they may see your good deeds and glorify your Father in heaven" (Matt. 5:16).

Validation in Christ

It's natural for children to love praise, but we must help them understand that their validation does not come from anything they do or the praise of others, but from God. In the book of John, Jesus said, "I have testimony weightier than that of John. For the works that the Father has given me to finish—the very works that I am doing—testify that the Father has sent me. And the Father who sent me has himself testified concerning me" (5:36–37). Jesus was saying that while John the Baptist spoke of him and Jesus spoke of himself as Savior and performed miracles, his validation came not from those things, but from the Father.

We want to convey to our children the example Jesus set for us all, which is that our validation is not real or satisfying if it is coming from other people patting us on the back or even in our own accomplishments or achievements. Just as God the Father validated Jesus when he said, "This is my Son, whom I love; with him I am well pleased" (Matt. 3:17), so does our validation come through Jesus, whose atonement for our sins enables us to hear in our hearts the voice of our Father saying, "Well done, good and faithful servant" (25:21).

Bragging on ourselves or glorying in other people bragging on us does not bring validation or stability of any kind. It is the work of Christ that makes our validation satisfying and secure. Jesus is the only validation that makes our lives truly appealing, fruitful, and effective. To bring this truth home to your child, you might say something like, "Sweetheart, when you brag on yourself or have a deep need for others to brag on you, it won't bring real happiness to your heart. Only Jesus can do that. He loves you so much that he died for you. It is his work in and through you that makes you special, not what you do or what is said about you. When you praise him instead of yourself, that brings him glory and makes him happy. When you bring him glory, he puts real joy in your heart too."

My husband and I look for every opportunity to encourage our children to live in complete dependence on our Lord for their validation, not seeking the approval of men and not fishing for compliments, but seeking to be a reflection of Jesus for the purpose of his glory.

Arguing

Katie's grades are dropping. Two of her teachers have already called her parents in for meetings, reporting that she is sleeping in class, turning in sloppy classwork and half-finished homework papers, not scoring as high as she usually does on tests, and not participating in class discussions. Katie has always made good grades in the past, has had no trouble focusing, and has never shown any signs of a learning disability. Mom is determined to get to the bottom of Katie's sudden change in academic achievements.

Mom steps into Katie's room and finds her propped on a pillow on her bed, engrossed in a book. After reporting the information obtained from Katie's teachers, Mom asks, "Sweetheart, has something been bothering you that you need to talk about? You've never been characterized by half-hearted schoolwork or study habits."

Katie lowers her book and replies, "No, nothing is wrong.

I've just really gotten into reading fiction books lately. The series I'm reading now is completely awesome. I'm having a hard time putting it down. Sometimes, I can't go to sleep for wondering what will happen next, so I get out my book light and read until I get sleepy. It's usually after midnight before I stop reading and go to sleep."

"Well, reading is great, honey, and I am glad you are enjoying it," Mom responds, "but we need to set some boundaries so your schoolwork doesn't suffer. I have noticed that you come in from school, go straight to your room, and start reading. It has obviously become a priority over your homework."

Katie sits up straighter in bed. "Our teachers encourage us to read rather than watching television because it is a healthier form of entertainment. So, really, you should be happy I am reading all the time instead of watching television."

"I agree with your teachers, Katie, and I just said I am glad you are enjoying reading, but we still need to set boundaries so that your grades don't suffer," explains Mom.

Mom continues with a plan. "I know you need a break from schoolwork when you first get home. I think it would be reasonable to read for an hour when you get home from school. Then after dinner and some family time, you should go ahead and do your homework and study. You need to be asleep by ten so that you aren't sleepy in class. If you finish everything by nine thirty, you can read an extra thirty minutes."

"What?" Katie blurts. "That is completely unreasonable! I've been reading at least three hours every night! An hour and a half is not enough time! I can't believe you are actually going to limit something that is good for me!"

Mom finds it difficult to understand why Katie is being so

argumentative and defensive over this issue. *I have tried to reason with her, while respecting and appreciating her desire to read,* Mom thinks to herself. *Why does she quickly resist everything I say? Why can't Katie see that I am offering a balanced plan? Why can't she just be more agreeable?*

Understand the Heart of the Matter

We should not be surprised when children sinfully resist our authority by means of arguing. Like every human, they are born sinners (Ps. 51:5). Therefore, they will manifest sinful behavior. The question we need to ask is not *Why do they behave this way?* but rather *How might I point them to their need for Christ and his power to change their lives?*

As explained in the introduction to this book, it is natural for children to sin (Rom. 3:23). At the heart of a child who is being argumentative and defensive is an unwillingness to submit to parental authority, which is ultimately an unwillingness to submit to God, the one who has placed parents as an authority over children. Just as God calls attempts to manipulate parental authority foolishness (see chapter 6 on manipulation), he also calls the resistance to parental authority foolishness: "A fool spurns a parent's discipline" (Prov. 15:5). Because he tells us that "folly is bound up in the heart of a child" (22:15), we should not be surprised when that folly manifests itself. It is the parent's responsibility to point children to their need for Christ in order that he might drive that foolishness out of their hearts and draw them to himself.

Ask Heart-Probing Questions

As you start the bigger conversation with your child, direct the focus away from the outward behavior of arguing and being defensive and focus on the inward issue of foolishness, which is a spiritual act of disobedience. In this case, Mom might redirect by asking, "Katie, is your argumentative and defensive attitude showing respect for me and honoring Jesus?" Rather than being drawn into an endless cycle of trying to reason with Katie and arguing back and forth, you might help her to consider and evaluate the spiritual choice she is making by asking, "Do you think it is wise or foolish for you to reject my instruction?"

Reprove Your Child for Foolishness

The book of Proverbs offers many warnings against resisting instruction. When children argue and defend their position as being right rather than heeding the counsel of their parents, it is considered foolishness according to Proverbs 12:15: "The way of fools seems right to them." To move into biblical correction, you might say, "Sweetheart, it is foolish to argue and disregard my instruction just so you can have your way. Proverbs 1:7 says, 'Fools despise wisdom and instruction.' I want to encourage you to desire to live in the wisdom of God, which is demonstrated in obeying and accepting the instruction of your parents."

Train Your Child in Wisdom

In contrast to the foolish child, who does not listen to advice and argues in order to live life however he wants, is the wise child, who realizes that God offers guidance for living through parental advice and instruction. To convey this truth to your child, you might say, "Honey, God desires for you to live wisely, not foolishly. We are told in Scripture that to be counted among the wise, we are to listen to advice and accept instruction" (Prov. 19:20).

Why Discipline a Child for Foolish Behavior?

Sometimes it is especially difficult to discipline a child for foolish behavior, especially when the behavior itself is the child refusing to listen to you. It can be easy to want to give up or let her argue with you as if she were your peer, especially with today's culture of friendship parenting. But we need to hold steady and discipline our children for their foolishness. Why?

Because it is a biblical command: Proverbs 22:6 commands parents, "Start children off on the way they should go, and even when they are old they will not turn from it." When the wise are trained by discipline, they grow up respecting their parents and God's wisdom. God uses discipline and instruction from parents as tools to impart wisdom. Proverbs 29:15 says, "A rod and a reprimand impart wisdom, but a child left undisciplined disgraces its mother." While our children do have a choice, and not all choose wisely, we are still commanded to do our part to discipline and instruct.

Because we love our children: Many parents have abandoned discipline and bought into modern psychology, believing that disciplining their children will scar them for life and diminish their creative, independent thinking. They say, "I love my children too much to discipline them." Solomon disagreed and taught that discipline is a necessary part of showing love to our children: "Whoever spares the rod hates their children, but the one who loves their children is careful to discipline them" (Prov. 13:24). Notice how Solomon used the word *careful.* Discipline is not to be a reactive, angry form of abuse, but a careful, controlled act of love toward our children.

While children do not enjoy the discipline itself, they are wise to accept the instruction of their parents and recognize that it is administered out of genuine love and concern for their well-being. Hebrews 12:6–11 beautifully explains this loving discipline:

> "The Lord disciplines the one he loves, and he chastens everyone he accepts as his son." Endure hardship as discipline; God is treating you as his children. For what children are not disciplined by their father? If you are not disciplined—and everyone undergoes discipline—then you are not legitimate, not true sons and daughters at all. Moreover, we have all had human fathers who disciplined us and we respected them for it. How much more should we submit to the Father of spirits and live! They disciplined us for a little while as they thought best; but God disciplines us for our good, in order that we may share in his holiness. No discipline seems pleasant at the

time, but painful. Later on, however, it produces a harvest of righteousness and peace for those who have been trained by it.

Because we desire what is best for our children: We want our children to avoid the consequences of foolish choices and experience the blessed peace and safety of walking in the wisdom of God. That wisdom comes from listening and practicing his commands. In comparing the blessings of those who live wisely with the consequences of those who live foolishly, Jesus said,

> Therefore everyone who hears these words of mine and puts them into practice is like a wise man who built his house on the rock. The rain came down, the streams rose, and the winds blew and beat against that house; yet it did not fall, because it had its foundation on the rock. But everyone who hears these words of mine and does not put them into practice is like a foolish man who built his house on sand. The rain came down, the streams rose, and the winds blew and beat against that house, and it fell with a great crash. (Matt. 7:24–27)

In desiring our children to love God, we should point them to their need for him by instructing and disciplining when they behave foolishly. Parents have a God-given responsibility to discipline their children for the foolishness of not listening and obeying instruction. We discipline out of a loving desire for our children to come into a dependent relationship with Jesus Christ and experience the spiritual peace and safety of knowing, loving, listening to, and following him. "Whoever listens to me will live in safety and be at ease, without fear of harm" (Prov. 1:33). There is no better, safer place for our children to dwell than in the will of God, regardless of what is happening in this world. In his will is the blessed assurance of his good plans for our children unfolding in this life, as well as the eternal life to come.

Therefore, we must encourage them and point them to Jesus through wise parenting. Wise children accept and respect the wisdom of God's Word. They believe in the consequences of disobedience and the blessings of obedience. "Whoever scorns instruction will pay for it, but whoever respects a command is rewarded" (13:13). Wise parents will take time to discipline and instruct their children in the ways of the Lord with the prayerful hope that they will recognize and surrender to their need for Jesus. May we, and our children, seek God's help in staying away from foolish ways and striving to love and embrace the wisdom and correction of the Lord.

THERE IS NO BETTER, SAFER PLACE FOR OUR CHILDREN TO DWELL THAN IN THE WILL OF GOD, REGARDLESS OF WHAT IS HAPPENING IN THIS WORLD.

YELLING

Dad unties his orange and blue apron and cheerfully calls everyone to the kitchen table for blueberry pancakes and bacon—a Saturday morning family tradition. Dad is hoping Eric will be in a better mood as he has been yelling at his sister and rolling his eyes at everything Mom and Dad have said all morning.

"Eric, did you finish cleaning your room before bed last night?" Mom calmly asks as she passes him the hot syrup.

"No, Mom, I didn't!" explodes Eric. "It's the weekend, and I really don't want to spend it cleaning my room!"

"Eric," Dad scolds. "Stop yelling at your mother! She asked you a simple question. You don't need to get so angry."

"I just want to rest on Saturdays! I'm sick and tired of you guys riding me all the time about cleaning my room and doing chores and homework and everything else. I just want everyone to leave me alone!" Eric yells as he slams his glass on the table so hard that orange juice splashes over the rim and pools onto the place mat.

"That's enough," Mom retorts. "Why can't we just enjoy our breakfast and talk like a normal family without your angry outbursts? I don't know what your problem is, Eric, but there is no excuse for your anger, so you can stop that yelling and straighten up right now."

"If you and Dad would just leave me alone, I wouldn't be so angry!" shouts Eric. "I just want to sleep in and play my video games and chill out on Saturdays. Is that too much to ask? I have to get up early every morning and I'm stressed out with school all week, then I have to be lectured by you guys all weekend. My life sucks! Just get off my back!"

Dad's face reddens as he pushes his chair from the table, stands up, throws his napkin onto his plate, and yells, "And you think we don't have busy, stressful lives too? We look forward to enjoying the weekends also, but your angry outbursts and rotten attitude make that pretty much impossible. We have to deal with things we don't enjoy doing all the time, but we don't take it out on you by yelling at you over Saturday morning breakfast!"

"Well, actually, Dad, you *are* yelling at me over Saturday morning breakfast," Eric says with a smirk.

Understand the Heart of the Matter

Since the heart is the foundation of behavior, we must understand that when our children express anger in sinful ways like yelling, they are drawing from what is in their hearts. We are told in Proverbs 4:23, "Above all else, guard your heart, for everything you do flows from it." The heart is the well from which all the responses to life gush forth. The anger a child exhibits is an expression of the overflow of the heart.

Anger is often a response to pain. Life stressors, such as school expectations, moving, divorce, the death of a loved one (including a family pet or close friend), just to name a few, can cause deep pain in a child and manifest itself through anger. Anger can be likened to a blinking light on the dashboard of a car, which alerts you that something is wrong under the hood. A wise parent will not ignore the warning signs or minimize the child's anger but will seek to understand and offer guidance.

It is easy to get into the habit of talking *to* our children, rather than talking *with* our children. We can become so adamant that our children listen to and understand us that we fail to listen to and understand them. Proverbs 18:2 warns against this sort of communication: "Fools find no pleasure in understanding but delight in airing their own opinions." We are also warned in Proverbs that "to answer before listening—that is folly and shame" (18:13). These verses confirm to parents that the finest art in communicating is not in learning how to express our thoughts and feelings but in learning how to draw out the thoughts and feelings of our children.

Our objective in communicating with an angry child must not be to tell him how we feel about his angry outbursts but to understand (and help him understand) the issues within his heart, which, in turn, helps him understand his need for Christ. When we lead our children to seek out what is in their hearts, we are teaching them to evaluate their own sinfulness, which will then lead them into a dependency on Jesus as they grow into adults.

In order for us to understand and help our children understand what is in their hearts, we have to develop our skills at probing the heart. We must learn how to get beyond the anger and yelling and help our children express what they are thinking and feeling. According to Proverbs, drawing out matters of the heart is not an easy task. "The purposes of a person's heart are deep waters, but one who has insight draws them out" (20:5). In asking for God's wisdom and guidance, we can all become skilled heart-probers.

Ask Heart-Probing Questions

As you think about approaching your angry child, remember that it is typically best to have the child cool off first, as there are chemical issues that occur within the body when anger is in full vent. These chemical reactions can greatly hinder the child's clear, rational thinking. Avoid trying to reason with an angry child as this can only escalate his anger to a level of higher intensity. Instead, you might say something along the lines of, "Honey, I can see that you are angry, and I want you to know it is not wrong for you to feel anger. Because I love you, I want to understand what is causing you to be so angry, but I won't be able to do that until you can talk with a voice as calm as mine. The best thing for us both is for you to go to your room and ask God to help you get control. Once you have calmed down, I would like for us to talk about what might be going on in your heart and how I can help you with that."

Once the child has calmed down and is ready to talk, you might begin the conversation with something like, "Sweetheart, when I asked if you had cleaned your room, what were you thinking and feeling that caused you to get so angry?" His response could reveal that his anger is rooted in hurt or frustration over something completely unrelated. It could also reveal that it is rooted in just plain laziness or outright defiance, to which you would address your response accordingly.

REPROVE YOUR CHILD FOR SINFUL ANGER

It is the parent's responsibility to reprove sinful anger in their children and help them understand that while God does give them the emotion of anger, they need to be careful not to dishonor God and their parents by expressing their anger in sinful ways.

In this case, Mom might say, "Eric, God gives many warnings about anger and reasons why it is foolish to give full vent to our rage (Prov. 29:11). Anger is a God-given emotion, but we are to avoid sinfully acting on that anger in a hotheaded or quick-tempered way, because it can lead us to do foolish things and sin in many other ways (14:16–17; 29:22). God desires you to live in accordance with his will. He says in James that 'human anger does not produce the righteousness that God desires'" (1:20).

TRAIN YOUR CHILD IN SELF-CONTROL

As parents desiring to encourage our children against the sinful expression of anger, we need to help them understand the benefits and blessings of replacing angry verbal responses with self-controlled verbal responses.

You might say, "Sweetheart, Dad and I desire you to experience the joy of God's presence and power in your life. We understand that there is some anger in your heart, and we very much want to understand it and help you deal with it in a way that honors Jesus and brings help and healing to you. We encourage you to pray and ask God to help you have the self-control to be 'quick to listen, slow to speak and slow to become angry' (James 1:19) while Dad and I are talking with you. With God's help, we can grow closer to him and one another as we work through this."

TEACH YOUR CHILD TO EXPRESS ANGER APPROPRIATELY

Anger can be a difficult issue to address in parenting. Demanding that our children not become angry can exasperate them and lead to emotionally unhealthy adults who struggle with guilt. We all experience feelings of anger. People and life in general can be hurtful and frustrating. Learning how to seek God in dealing with the emotion of anger biblically equips children to become Christ-dependent adults who experience his power made perfect through weakness.

It was not necessarily wrong that Eric experienced feelings of angry frustration when his parents asked about cleaning his room. Eric could have responded to his anger with self-control. It is always wise to step back and take some time when anger surfaces rather than losing control. Holding our tongues, walking away if necessary, and asking God to empower us with self-control keeps us from becoming enslaved to our emotions and enables us to walk in the power and freedom of Christ.

During a time of non-conflict, discussing a means of escape with your child can be helpful. Something along the lines of "I can feel myself getting angry. I need to take some time to pray and calm down before we discuss this any further" is an adequate means of escape for both the parent and the child.

Discussing the difference in how Eric *could have responded* to his anger would be beneficial in equipping him to demonstrate self-control in similar situations in the future. Once Eric calmed down, he could have come back and calmly said something such as, "Mom, I know you asked me to clean my room before bed last night, and I'm sorry I didn't. I was so tired. I've had a hard and stressful week. Would it be okay if I just chilled out and played some video games after breakfast, and then after lunch I'll clean my room?"

> HOLDING OUR TONGUES, WALKING AWAY IF NECESSARY, AND ASKING GOD TO EMPOWER US WITH SELF-CONTROL KEEPS US FROM BECOMING ENSLAVED TO OUR EMOTIONS AND ENABLES US TO WALK IN THE POWER AND FREEDOM OF CHRIST.

Dealing with anger biblically is just one of the many opportunities we have to seek and respond to God's will in our lives. Asking for and receiving God's power to help us live in accordance with his will is how we grow in the righteousness of Christ. It is how we become more like him and bring him the glory he deserves.

Is Anger Sinful?

As you work through deeper issues with children struggling with anger, the question might come up regarding how sinful an emotion can be. The Bible does not say, "Do not become angry."

What it does say is, "In your anger do not sin" (Eph. 4:26). Children need to understand that anger is an emotion given to us by God, but it can become sinful when it is expressed in the form of outwardly attacking another person, which was the case with Eric in this chapter's opening scenario.

The other way anger becomes sinful that children need to understand is when it dwells within the heart and grows into a root of bitterness, which is why we are told in Ephesians to "get rid of all bitterness, rage and anger" (v. 31). We should teach our children to deal with anger promptly as it is through the neglect of addressing it quickly and biblically that they are prone to become enslaved to it. This is why God's children are warned, "Do not let the sun go down while you are still angry" (v. 26). We should warn that if they wait, they could wind up being in bondage to their anger, which could lead to other sins, as it did with Cain in the book of Genesis. When Cain allowed his anger toward his brother Abel to grow, he wound up murdering him (Gen. 4).

You might communicate to your children the importance of dealing with anger by saying something like, "Honey, God says we are to get rid of anger in our hearts quickly so that it doesn't lead to other sins and make our hearts bitter and hard. If you ask God to help you get rid of the anger in your heart, he will."

If children do not learn how to deal with their anger, it can become a monster that reaps devastation and destruction on their lives. However, when they learn to depend on and trust God regardless of how they feel, it can lead to tremendous blessings in their lives and the lives of others, just as it did with Joseph in the book of Genesis (chapter 50). Consider reminding them about the story of Joseph again and all the blessings that came from Joseph honoring God with his responses. You might say, "After Joseph's brothers betrayed him and sold him into slavery, I would imagine Joseph struggled with anger toward his brothers and the unfairness of the whole situation. Yet, Joseph trusted and depended on God rather than allowing his feelings to rule him. As a result, he, his family, and an entire nation prospered."

Respect Your Child's Feelings

If we are seeking to unpack the emotion of anger with our kids, we need to create an environment where they will feel safe to address their emotions. Most children will talk openly about their feelings when parents express a genuine interest in understanding and respecting what they have to say. When we approach our children in a nonthreatening, open manner and recognize their feelings as valid, they are much more likely to trust us with their hearts. Once trust and respect are established, the doors of communication open, and opportunity arises for working toward a solution, especially when the child is given a voice in the solution. A simple statement such as, "Would there have been a time or way that I could have asked about cleaning your room that would have been better for you?" exemplifies humility, sensitivity, and a willingness to admit that you do not always get it right either.

Let your children know you are human, too, and demonstrate how dependent you are on Christ for your own issues with anger. Offer examples of times you were angry and how you responded. Personal testimony of Christ's work in our lives is a powerful thing. Tell about a time when you became enslaved to anger and the consequences that resulted, as well as a time when you trusted God and responded in obedience. Discuss how the choices we make in responding to anger determine the consequences we suffer or the victory in Christ we enjoy. Encourage your child to use anger as a means to draw closer to God and experience the richness of his power and freedom.

GOSSIPING

Mom is listening to her two daughters chat on the swing set while she washes the outside windows of the house. "Did you hear about Julie Thompson yelling at Randy Parker on the field trip last week?" Amber asks her sister, Cindy, as she straightens her legs, leans back, and propels her swing to go higher.

Cindy looks down from the top of the slide and replies, "No, but Julie has always been mean, so I'm not surprised. Why was she yelling at him?"

"Well," Amber says with a grin, eager to give her sister the scoop, "I heard that Randy was telling people that Julie told Hudson that she liked him. She was probably mad that Randy was telling people about it."

"What?" Cindy asks with an appalled expression. "She said she likes Hudson? I heard she told Troy Radcliff that she liked him at the homecoming dance last month, and I know she was holding hands with Jason Harper on the back of the bus when school first started. She is just going from one guy to the next."

"Yeah, I know," replies Amber. "There's no telling what else she's done. I can't stand girls like that!"

"Girls," Mom gently rebukes. "You shouldn't be talking bad about that poor girl. You don't know what might be going on in her life. Her parents are getting a divorce, so she's probably going through a lot right now. Maybe you girls should befriend and encourage her rather than spreading rumors about her."

"Oh, Mom, you totally don't get it. Julie is mean, and she is obviously getting a bad reputation now too. Why would we want to be friends with someone like that?"

"Well, whether you choose to be friends with her or not, you need to stop being judgmental and gossiping about her," Mom demands.

"Okay," the girls reply in unison.

"We'll stop talking about her," Cindy adds, then leans over and whispers to Amber, "that is, we'll stop talking about her in front of Mom!"

"Yeah," Amber whispers back with a conspiring wink. "We'll talk about it later."

Understand the Heart of the Matter

We must understand that judging and gossiping, like all sins, come from within. Jesus said, "For it is from within, out of a person's heart, that evil thoughts come—sexual immorality, theft, murder, adultery, greed, malice, deceit, lewdness, envy, slander, arrogance and folly. All these evils come from inside and defile a person" (Mark 7:21–23).

The "from within" part of that verse tells us that outward

behaviors are only the manifestations of the real problem, which is in the heart. The Bible uses the heart to speak of the inner you. The heart is the control center of life. Certainly, behavior is what alerts us to a child's need for correction, but we must be careful not to make the mistake of allowing the desire for *changed behavior* to substitute for the desire for a *changed heart.*

Keep in mind that our children may change their behavior to that which is acceptable, especially while we are watching, but there may not be an actual heart change taking place. A change in behavior that does not stem from a change in heart is not commendable; it is condemnable. It is based on the same sort of hypocrisy that Jesus condemned in the Pharisees. He said that they honored him with their lips, but their hearts were far from him. Jesus labeled them as people who washed the outside of the cup while the inside was still unclean (Luke 11:39).

> WE MUST BE CAREFUL NOT TO MAKE THE MISTAKE OF ALLOWING THE DESIRE FOR *CHANGED BEHAVIOR* TO SUBSTITUTE FOR THE DESIRE FOR A *CHANGED HEART.*

When we focus on our children's outward behavior only, neglecting what is on the inside, we can cause our children to become manipulators. They may learn how to please us outwardly, often out of a fear of punishment, but they do not learn the righteousness of Christ or how utterly dependent they are on him. Also, when we only focus on teaching them proper outward behavior but fail to train their hearts in accordance with God's Word and point them to their need for Jesus, we risk them viewing Christianity as a strict, nitpicking religion that is made up of nothing but legalistic rules. As a result, they may never experience what it means to truly know Christ and his power to transform lives. We must understand, and help our children understand, that it is their straying hearts that have *resulted* in wrong behavior and that Jesus Christ is the only help and cure for sin.

At the heart of judging and gossiping is a sinfully distorted view of oneself and God. In other words, we think too highly of ourselves and we do not think highly enough of God. When the people condemned a woman caught in adultery and wanted to stone her, Jesus said, "Let any one of you who is without sin be the first to throw a stone at her" (John 8:7). The people thought far too highly of themselves, determining that they were righteous enough to pass judgment and administer consequences. Jesus caused them to look inside themselves, which quickly set them all straight. In revealing that none is without sin, Jesus validated that no one except our holy God has the right to judge.

Jesus said that judgmental actions derive from a heart of hypocrisy, and he warned the self-appointed judges who thought so highly of themselves:

Do not judge, or you too will be judged. For in the same way you judge others, you will be judged, and with the measure you use, it will be measured to you. Why do you look at the speck of sawdust in your brother's eye and pay no attention to the plank in your own eye? How can you say to your brother, 'Let me take the speck out of your eye,' when all the time there is a plank in your own eye? You hypocrite, first take the plank out of your own eye, and then you will see clearly to remove the speck from your brother's eye. (Matt. 7:1–5)

Judgment and gossip typically go hand in hand, as gossip is birthed from a heart of judgment. The heart nurtures and grows a seed of judgment, then the mouth spews out the venomous results, slanderously showing others in a shameful or negative light. The apostle James gave strong warning against judging and gossiping: "Brothers and sisters, do not slander one another. Anyone who speaks against a brother or sister or judges them speaks against the law and judges it. When you judge the law, you are not keeping it, but sitting in judgment on it" (James 4:11).

James was referring to the law of love spoken of in Galatians 5:14: "For the entire law is fulfilled in keeping this one command: 'Love your neighbor as yourself.'" James was warning that if we judge and gossip about others, then we are not being obedient to the law of love that God sets forth in Scripture.

Thinking and spreading negative or shameful information about another person is contrary to walking in love the way we are told to in 1 Corinthians 13:

Love is patient, love is kind. It does not envy, it does not boast, it is not proud. It does not dishonor others, it is not self-seeking, it is not easily angered, it keeps no record of wrongs. Love does not delight in evil but rejoices with the truth. It always protects, always trusts, always hopes, always perseveres (vv. 4–7).

Contrary to judgment and gossip, love thinks no evil, speaks no evil, listens to no evil, and believes the best about others. Therefore, we want to help our children understand that it is through loving, accepting, and serving others with the strength of Christ that we please and honor God.

Ask Heart-Probing Questions

Help your child understand that sinners do not have the right to judge other sinners or gossip about them. You might start with, "Sweetheart, the Bible says that we are all sinners in need of God's mercy and grace. We are to show the same mercy and grace to others that God shows to us. Do you think that what you are saying about Julie honors the God who created her? How do you think God feels about Julie? Are the words you are saying about Julie demonstrating the mercy and grace that God offers?"

Reprove Your Child for Gossiping and Judging

There are so many biblical warnings regarding gossiping and judging and what those sins can lead to. It is wise for parents to convey those warnings to their children.

You might say, "God is not glorified when we judge others and spread gossip about them. The Bible warns that we will be judged in the same way and with the same measure that we judge others (Matt. 7:1–2). In the book of Leviticus we are given the command to 'not go about spreading slander' (19:16) and in Proverbs we are told that whoever 'spreads slander is a fool'" (10:18).

Train Your Child to Love Others

In the pursuit of showing love to others, the tongue plays an important role. While it does have the power to destroy, it also has the power to heal, comfort, nurture, and edify the people around us. In encouraging your child to love others, you might say, "Honey, because our words are so powerful, we should choose them carefully and use them to love others by building them up and saying things that benefit them (Eph. 4:29). In the book of Titus, we are encouraged to be peaceable, considerate, and gentle toward everyone (3:2), and 1 Peter 3:8 tells us to be sympathetic and compassionate, to show love and to be humble toward others."

The Destructive Nature of Gossip

With our human tendency to measure sin, with some being much worse than others, it might be easy to play off just how destructive gossip can be. We may reason that gossip is a lesser sin, but it is all sin in the eyes of the Lord and can be just as destructive as any other.

Kids often reason along the same lines as adults when it comes to the seriousness of gossip. Gossip may not always seem like a big deal to our kids, especially with all the unexpected ways it permeates our lives, and this can make it a difficult issue to address. But we need to help our children understand how the Bible warns of the alluring yet destructive nature of gossip. "The words of a gossip are like choice morsels; they go down to the inmost parts" (Prov. 18:8).

Whether we admit it or not, there is something intriguing about gossip. Television is saturated with gossipy talk shows, and grocery store checkout racks are overstuffed with magazine tabloids that entice our fascination with gossip. Proverbs confirms that gossip is like a tasty morsel that we like to savor. It's like an all-you-can-eat buffet bar with all our favorites, from lobster and steak to peach cobbler and banana pudding. We cannot get enough. And the temptation to gossip begins young.

Proverbs warns not only that we have a corrupt attraction to gossip, but also of the damaging effects. It says when we listen to and absorb gossip, it goes to our "inmost parts." Gossip sinks its teeth into our hearts, souls, and minds and poisons us like a fast-spreading cancer. Its effects reveal themselves spiritually and emotionally and make their mark on the gossiper, the listener, and the victim.

GOSSIP DAMAGES THE GOSSIPER

In talking about the evils of the tongue, James said, "It corrupts the whole body, sets the whole course of one's life on fire, and is itself set on fire by hell" (3:6). Proverbs also speaks of the consequences of an unrestrained tongue: "Those who speak rashly will come to ruin" (13:3). To speak thoughtlessly, carelessly, and recklessly about others not only makes us an accomplice to sinful gossip fueled by hell, but also corrupts our whole bodies and sets our lives on a foolish, destructive course.

You might convey this truth to your child by saying, "Honey, when something bad pops into your mind about someone, it is better to confess that thought to God rather than say it. When you confess bad thoughts about someone else to God and ask him to make your heart right, he does, and he keeps the sin of gossip from corrupting your whole body and causing trouble in your life."

GOSSIP DAMAGES THE LISTENER

Gossip also damages the person hearing the gossip, for it entices him or her to judge and gossip as well. So if we're not the one originating the gossip but are listening to it, that doesn't let us off the hook. When we allow gossip even to be spoken to us, there is the potential for corruption.

Another danger of listening to gossip is that it could lead to the hurtful ending of a friendship. Gossip separates people and even destroys relationships. As Proverbs says, "A perverse person stirs up conflict, and a gossip separates close friends" (16:28).

Since we are commanded not to judge or gossip (James 4:11), we must teach our children to make every effort to avoid participating in these sins—even to the point of refusing to listen. If the gossiper cannot be persuaded to stop, children should be taught that it may be necessary to walk away to avoid involvement in sinful conversation. Proverbs reiterates the wisdom of walking away and not participating in gossip: "A gossip betrays a confidence; so avoid anyone who talks too much" (20:19).

To communicate these truths to your children, you might say, "The Bible says 'bad company corrupts good character' (1 Cor. 15:33), and when someone is talking badly about someone else, they are being bad company. So, to avoid the temptation of listening to gossip and allowing your own heart to be corrupted, it would be wise not to listen, even if you have to walk away."

Gossip Damages the Victim

Our children need to realize that while the tongue is only a small part of the body, it is extremely powerful. In the book of James it is compared to a fire (3:5). Just as a small spark can ignite and destroy an entire forest, so can the fiery darts of the tongue destroy those we are called to love according to God's good purpose. The tongue's power to destroy others is confirmed in Proverbs 18:21: "The tongue has the power of life and death."

Anyone who has suffered the agony of being gossiped about understands just how hurtful it can be and probably has a deeper respect for the command to "Do to others as you would have them do to you" (Luke 6:31). The old sticks-and-stones saying does not ring true to one who has been pierced by the sharp arrow of painful gossip. No one wishes to be the subject of gossip. Slanderous words hurt and destroy.

You might communicate these truths to your children by telling them about a time you or someone you know was hurt by gossip. You can also ask your children if they or others they know have ever been hurt by gossip. Discuss the specific, hurtful feelings that resulted to help them come to an even deeper understanding of gossip's destructive nature.

Honor the Lord—Nip Judgment and Gossip in the Bud!

Because judgment and gossip dishonor God, we are to quickly nip them in the bud. It is easy to make excuses such as, "If I'm telling the truth, it is not judging or gossiping." There is no excuse according to the apostle Paul. "You, therefore, have no excuse, you who pass judgment on someone else, for at whatever point you judge another, you are condemning yourself, because you who pass judgment do the same things" (Rom. 2:1).

This verse has rung true for me on more occasions than I care to tell you about. It would take more than my fingers and toes to count how many times I have judged someone for something "I would never do" only to wind up doing it myself. There is no getting around the truth of God's Word. A follower of Jesus should not judge and should not spread gossip. Gossip is a parasite. In order for a parasite to live, it requires a host organism. Christians should not give gossip a place to live or breed. So, as you talk with your children about this, vaccinate them with scriptures. Encourage them to pray, and ask God to help them avoid these poisonous sins of the heart. Injections of biblical truth and strong doses of the Holy Spirit can control the deadly viruses of judgment and gossip, making your children, those around them, and the body of Christ a whole lot healthier.

Encourage your kids to consider Proverbs 26:20 whenever they are tempted to gossip and judge: "Without wood a fire goes out; without a gossip a quarrel dies down." Teach them how to turn the tables on those who try to gossip by redirecting the conversation to something that edifies the person being talked about. In this way they will honor the Lord with their words. Train your children to respond biblically by encouraging the gossiper to befriend and reach out to others who may be hurting or making bad choices. Loving responses will glorify God, benefit all involved, and smother the fires of judgment and gossip before the corruption spreads.

It is as Peter said, "If anyone speaks, they should do so as one who speaks the very words of God. If anyone serves, they should do so with the strength God provides, so that in all things God may be praised through Jesus Christ. To him be the glory and the power for ever and ever. Amen" (1 Peter 4:11).

BICKERING

Josh and his sister Cathy are toe-to-toe in a heated argument in Josh's room. Mom can feel the tension as she walks down the hall with a laundry basket of clean clothes. Mom lets out an exhausted sigh as she props the laundry basket on her hip and leans her back against the wall just outside Josh's bedroom door.

Earlier that morning, Mom had run the siblings out of the living room because they were arguing over which Saturday morning cartoon to watch. By lunch, they were still arguing over everything from which flavor jelly was better on peanut butter sandwiches to whose backyard fort was cooler. Mom became so annoyed listening to their constant bickering that she had both children leave the table at lunch with their plates, sentencing them to their own bedrooms to finish their pizza roll-ups alone. Now here it is mid-afternoon, and they are still at each other's throats.

"It was not Pluto! It was Goofy!" yells Josh. "I remember because we had just gotten off that stupid teacup ride where Snow White was sitting in the cup beside us!"

"You're wrong!" insisted Cathy, her voice even louder than Josh's. "It was not Goofy! It may have been after the teacup ride, but Goofy was not the one on the merry-go-round with us! It was Pluto! You don't ever remember anything right. I am sure it was Pluto because the little girl on the horse beside me was so scared of him that she was clinging to her dad. She wouldn't have been scared of Goofy because he's so silly looking. It was Pluto!"

"No," retorts Josh. "You are the one that's not remembering it right. He had on a green hat like Goofy wears. Pluto never wears a hat. You are totally wrong like you always are. It was Goofy!"

"*Mooom!*" Cathy comes running out of Josh's room and stops short when she sees Mom propped against the hallway wall with a frown on her face.

"I heard the whole thing, Cathy," Mom says with a groan as she hands the basket of clothes to her. "Go put these in your room. I'm sick of listening to the two of you argue over every little thing. What difference does it make if it was Goofy or Pluto?"

Hearing Cathy recruit Mom into the debate, Josh stomps into the hall and says, "Mom, you remember that it was Goofy on the merry-go-round in Disney World last year, right? Tell Cathy it was Goofy and not Pluto."

Frustrated, Mom throws her hands up in the air, turns on her heels, and heads back down the hall as she retorts, "No, Josh, I don't remember which one it was, and I don't care. What I do care about is that the two of you are constantly arguing and driving me crazy! Stop arguing!"

Understand the Heart of the Matter

Like most sins, pride is typically at the root of arguing. We are told in Proverbs, "Where there is strife, there is pride" (13:10). Being right feels better than being wrong, so there is a great temptation to puff up with pride and "fight to be right" about even trivial issues, as was the case in the opening scenario with Josh and Cathy. Pride also feeds selfishness as we strive to gain something over another or come out better than someone else. This is demonstrated when siblings quarrel over issues such as who gets the biggest piece of cake, who gets to ride in the front seat, or who gets to sleep on the top bunk.

Today's culture would like for us to believe that it is normal for siblings not to get along and not to like each other. This is readily seen in the media. Rarely do movie or television siblings treat one another with respect and affection. They are usually fighting and yelling at each other. And it is all portrayed as not only okay, but expected. In a Christian home, however, it should not be accepted or waved off. Quarreling among siblings should be viewed as valuable opportunities to teach them about the commands of Christ to "love one another" and "put others above ourselves."

Naturally, siblings are going to argue and get on one another's nerves from time to time, but it is important that parents cultivate into their children's hearts the qualities of love, humility, gentleness, self-control, and peacemaking, which are theirs in Christ Jesus. When siblings learn to take hold of these qualities offered to them through Jesus, they experience the transforming power of the gospel in their own hearts and in their relationships with one another.

Ask Heart-Probing Questions

As you approach children who are quarreling with each other and seek to help them look deeper, you might begin by offering wisdom from Proverbs, saying something such as, "The Bible says that fools are quick to quarrel (20:3). It actually takes more strength to abstain from quarreling than to participate in it." You could then ask a few heart-probing questions and discuss them with the children together or individually. Questions that might be helpful for shedding light on healthy conflict resolution that honors God might be, "Are you being strong and avoiding strife, or are you being weak and participating in strife? Are you respecting each other and honoring God in the way you are speaking to each other? What can you say to keep peace with your brother (or sister) right now?"

Reprove Your Child for Quarreling

Parents are wise to teach their children what the Bible says about the root sin of quarreling and why they should avoid harsh words that stir up anger and conflict.

You might say, "The way you guys are talking to each other is harsh, and we are told in Proverbs that "a harsh word stirs up anger" (15:1). It also says in Proverbs that "hatred stirs up conflict" (10:12) and that those who choose to quarrel are choosing to love sin (17:19). At the heart of quarreling for the purpose of being right is pride (13:10), and pride does not honor God or show love for each other."

Train Your Child to Pursue Peace

Then, as you switch over from reproving to training, you might encourage your children with something such as, "When you speak gently to each other, anger will not flare up and things won't get so heated and out of control (15:1). It shows honor to avoid strife and quarreling (20:3), and it is a command of God that you make every effort to pursue and promote peace (Rom. 12:18). In showing the kind of love for one another that God desires, you should purpose in your heart not to repay insult with insult, but with blessing" (1 Peter 3:9).

Overlooking Minor Offenses

One part of talking with your kids about quarreling is helping them think through whether something is really worth arguing about. Proverbs tells us, "A person's wisdom yields patience; it is to one's glory to overlook an offense" (19:11). Encourage your children to patiently stop and consider before engaging in an argument. Teach them to weigh their response by thinking through some questions: Will this really matter tomorrow or next week? Is this an opportunity to be wise and overlook the difference of opinion or offense?

Paul offered wise instruction to Timothy when he said, "Don't have anything to do with foolish and stupid arguments, because you know they produce quarrels" (2 Tim. 2:23). Not only is quarreling derived from pride and hatred (Prov. 13:10; 10:12), but it can also wreak destruction on a relationship. Galatians tell us, "If you bite and devour each other, watch out or you will be destroyed by each other" (5:15).

Encourage your children to recognize and walk away from foolish disputes. Is not the relationship more important than being right over a frivolous issue? Wisdom is shown in dropping the issue before the damage is done. As Proverbs says, "Starting a quarrel is like breaching a dam; so drop the matter before a dispute breaks out" (17:14).

Resolving Conflict Biblically

Sometimes, though, we really must engage in conflict, and we need to teach our children how to handle it biblically, seeking opportunities to glorify God, serve others, and grow to be more like Christ. The secret to resolving a quarrel gracefully is to bleed Bible when pricked. Teach your children to hide God's Word in their hearts and to pray that the Holy Spirit will lead and strengthen them through the power of the gospel. When children are taught to seek a Christlike attitude toward conflict, it changes the way they view it and the way they handle it.

> THE SECRET TO RESOLVING A QUARREL GRACEFULLY IS TO BLEED BIBLE WHEN PRICKED.

In the book of Matthew, we are told to "Settle matters quickly" (5:25). Sometimes this can simply mean agreeing to disagree by dropping the matter and fleeing from the prideful temptation to merely "be right."

There are legitimate conflicts worthy of attention, but they are to be dealt with properly by demonstrating the qualities of a loving heart. Paul told us exactly what these qualities are in 1 Corinthians:

> Love is patient, love is kind. It does not envy, it does not boast, it is not proud. It does not dishonor others, it is not self-seeking, it is not easily angered, it keeps no record of wrongs. Love does not delight in evil but rejoices with the truth. It always protects, always trusts, always hopes, always perseveres. (13:4-7)

Resolving conflict biblically involves humility. True humility considers others better, puts the needs of others first (Phil. 2:3-4), and focuses on one's own wretchedness, rather than the wretchedness of others. Sincere humility can soften hearts and bring an argument to resolution more quickly. Therefore, we are instructed to "be completely humble and gentle; be patient, bearing with one another in love. Make every effort to keep the unity of the Spirit through the bond of peace" (Eph. 4:2-3). Be sure to point out the different outcomes your children experience when they speak to each other with humility and gentleness, rather than pride and anger, confirming that "those who promote peace have joy" (Prov. 12:20).

Encourage your children to work through conflicts and differences kindly, gently, humbly, and with a willingness to put the interests of others before their own. As they put these lessons into practice, they will learn that others are typically more agreeable to work out conflicts and differences peacefully when they are treated with love, respect, and kindness. They will find that as they bear with one another in love (Eph. 4:2), they enjoy a closer, more blessed relationship that honors God.

When children learn to seek the Lord for resolving conflict

biblically, their hearts are softened and awakened to the transforming power of the gospel. The psalmist said, "How good and pleasant it is when God's people live together in unity" (Ps. 133:1). Therefore, let us encourage our children to "make every effort to do what leads to peace and to mutual edification" (Rom. 14:19). May they learn to seek and depend completely on Jesus, who is the almighty source of strength, and may they experience and radiate the supreme work of Christ in their relationships, hearts, and lives.

What's a Good Parent to Do?

e all desire to be good parents. When we are old and gray, wouldn't it be nice to be able to look back on our parenting years with no regrets, breathe a contented sigh of relief, and say, "I was a good parent"? Realistically, there is no good in us apart from Christ, and although his goodness is ultimately victorious as we abide in him, we are still bound to make some mistakes in parenting. Thank God for his grace in covering our mistakes and even using them for his glory when we humble ourselves and learn from them. We can also be thankful for those who have gone before us and shared wisdom from their own failures and successes in parenting so that we, and our children, might benefit. Here are a few insightful tips I've learned from my mentors over the years.

Avoid Threatening and Repeating Instructions

It is so easy for us to fall into the trap of repeating instructions and making threats. After all, it can be quite tiring to take time to think through and faithfully instruct our children. So, we hope that if we just give them one more chance, they will comply. The threatening parent says, "If you don't start sharing your toys right now, I'm going to send them all off to kids who *will* share!" Yet, how many of those parents do you think actually packed up their kids' toys and shipped them off to Timbuktu? I seriously doubt many, if any. When threatening does not work, we typically go back to repeating, in hopes that eventually they will obey.

Repeating instructions again and again or making threats teaches children that Mom does not mean what she says. We should avoid saying things that we do not mean. When my children were younger, I remember needing a little time to unwind. I loved them with all my heart, but I just needed to get away sometimes. One of the things I always looked forward to was Tuesday nights. My parents, being wonderful, devoted grandparents, loved to have Wesley and Alex spend the night with them every Tuesday night. It was a huge blessing for us all that I never took for granted, as I know many do not have that luxury. I remember a particular Tuesday afternoon when I had instructed my children to clean their rooms and they didn't. All day I was anticipating a night of peace and quiet. Then, I heard the words coming out of my mouth, "If you don't get your rooms clean, you are not spending the night with Nana and Papa tonight." In reality, I knew good and well I was not about to forfeit my night of leisure by following through with that threat.

We are told in Matthew 5:37, "All you need to say is simply 'Yes' or 'No'; anything beyond this comes from the evil one." In other words, we are to simply let our yes be yes and our no be no.

We are to say what we mean and mean what we say, or we will exasperate our children. Not only does failing to comply with this biblical instruction cause confusion in our children, but it's hard to take a lying parent seriously.

I find it interesting that some of the most admirable and successful generals of our country all had one thing in common— they were certain of their commands before they issued them. They did not threaten. They did not repeat. Soldiers do not respect or respond well to an uncertain and inconsistent leader. Paul said it best in 1 Corinthians 14:8: "If the trumpet does not sound a clear call, who will get ready for battle?" Likewise, when Mom issues half-hearted commands to her children and does not require her children to follow through immediately, she sends mixed signals. Not only will this sort of leadership earn Mom the Most Wishy-Washy in Command medal, but it will also cause her children to question their own positions in the family. They will become uncertain of when and how to respond to Mom's instructions. This can lead to insecure children who are unsure of their own actions. When we lead our "troops" with confidence, however, they find security and stability in their call to obedience.

We should never issue a warning or a command without following it through. This rule of thumb requires that we think before we speak. Try not to say yes or no to something until you are sure that it is your definite answer. According to Proverbs, it is biblical that we not speak before thinking: "The heart of the righteous *weighs* its answers" (15:28, emphasis added). Let us weigh our answers, give confident commands, and raise up a mighty army for the Lord.

WHAT ABOUT CONSEQUENCES?

Perhaps one of the most difficult duties of a parent is the enforcement of consequences. To purposefully inflict any unpleasantry on our children is a hard thing to do. It goes against our natural instinct to protect those we love from any sort of pain or suffering.

We must realize that while administering consequences is not pleasant, it is a necessary part of discipline that leads to righteousness and peace. "No discipline seems pleasant at the time, but painful. Later on, however, it produces a harvest of righteousness and peace for those who have been trained by it" (Heb. 12:11). Consequences are part of God's ordained method for training children in righteousness. When parents administer consequences as part of discipline, children learn the law of the harvest. They learn that God has built the principle of sowing and reaping into their words.

I am going to tread lightly here, as God's specific instructions for parents to discipline their children with consequences is thoroughly covered in my other book, *"Don't Make Me Count to Three!"*[1] But I would like to briefly touch on the ineffectiveness of time-outs, as this has become a popular consequence, and I would also like to encourage parents to allow the punishment to fit the crime when possible.

In my opinion and experience, time-outs are ineffective, as they lead to power struggles. For example: Little Tommy directly disobeys Mom. Mom commands Tommy to sit in time-out, so he sits with arms folded and a pouty face for about thirty seconds. He tires of sitting and gets up. Mom makes him sit back down only to enter into a power struggle when he gets up again. Not only has the original issue of disobedience not been addressed as a problem of the heart, but now Mom has created a whole new issue of disobedience with which to deal. Be wiser than your child. Avoid power struggles.

Whenever possible, it is appropriate and effective to let the punishment fit the crime. When my son left his bike in the yard rather than returning it to the garage, he lost the freedom of enjoying his bike the next day. I said, "Sweetheart, I told you to put your bike away before you came in for the evening. Because I love you and want you to learn to be responsible and obey my instructions, you will not have the freedom to ride your bike tomorrow. Hopefully, that will help motivate you to be responsible and obey."

When my daughter did not clean her room after playtime, she lost the freedom to watch a show with her brother that night. I explained, "Honey, you did not obey and clean your room like I told you. I love you and want you to learn to obey, so you have lost the freedom to watch a show with your brother tonight." Help them understand that responsibility and obedience lead to freedom. Logical, related consequences are also effective for helping the forgetful child to remember.

Remind your child that whether or not there are consequences is her choice. Her response to your authority determines the outcome. You might say, "Sweetheart, it is my responsibility to administer consequences when you disobey, but whether you obey or disobey is completely your choice. In other words, when you disobey, you are choosing to have consequences."

Be sure not to overdo consequences. Grounding your children for weeks or months over one act of disobedience can exasperate them. Pray that God will make appropriate consequences clear to you.

It is important that you and your spouse discuss and pray

over consequences for areas with which your children struggle. It is imperative that you are on the same page, lest your children learn to manipulate you against each other. Children find security in knowing that Mom and Dad are unified in parenting. If you are single, let your children know that you are seeking God for wisdom in training them in his ways.

As you faithfully train and discipline your children through the use of consequences, especially on the days when you are exhausted or discouraged because it seems not to be making a difference, be encouraged with my favorite verse for parenting: "Let us not become weary in doing good, for at the proper time we will reap a harvest if we do not give up" (Gal. 6:9). There were so many days I remember clinging to that one.

Sow Now, Reap Later

Thorough and consistent training does take time, but taking time to train children to obey when they are younger can save years of battling disobedience as they grow older.

It is also better to train than to retrain. Many parents hold the reins loosely when children are younger, allowing them to get away with everything short of murder. Then they try to tighten the reins as their children get older. If five-year-old Jenny is allowed to disobey by not responding when you call her, but at seventeen she is grounded because she arrived home past her curfew, Jenny will more than likely become angry and rebel against the authority to which she is just now being required to submit. Ideally, it is best to hold the reins tightly during the younger years, diligently training your children in the ways of the Lord, asking

God to work through you to grow them in wisdom and stature. Then you will be able to loosen the reins as they move into the teen years and prove themselves mature and trustworthy.

Speak God's Word, Not Our Words

When we use God's Word rather than our words for training our children, we are relying on God's wisdom rather than our own. As we briefly touched on in chapter one, it is the power of God's Word, not ours, that exposes the wrong, convicts the guilty, and promotes righteousness. In order for children to receive God's grace and walk in his righteousness, they must first be convicted of their sins. They must admit they are guilty. God uses his Word to convict his children. Therefore, when our children sin, we should use God's Word in order that they might be convicted. Teaching our children in accordance with God's Word (God's law) shows them that they are sinners in need of God's mercy and intervention in their lives. Every time our children sin, we have a valuable opportunity to point them to their need for Christ.

We should not soften or make light of sin by addressing it and flippantly dismissing it as the world does. We should address it as God addresses it. We should call it what God calls it. In other words, we should not replace telling a lie with telling a "fib," being disrespectful with "acting ugly," being foolish with being "stubborn," or being disobedient with being "strong-willed." It is the convicting power of God's Holy Word and Spirit that brings about change.

Although many of the examples in this book pertain to younger children, the same biblical principles apply to older children. God's Word is profitable and beneficial for all ages. God's Word never changes. The way that sin manifests itself, however, changes as children get older. Aggravating, lying, complaining, manipulating, etc., may manifest differently with older children, but God's Word is always the same. Therefore, it should always be the living and active Word of God that we use for training them in the Lord's ways.

Some view training children in God's Word as being a formal, strict, or legalistic way of teaching. Others fear that feeding children God's Word as a means to train and discipline will cause them to view the Bible in a negative light. However, nothing could be further from the truth. Instilling scriptures into our children is a way of life, to be talked about during all occasions all the time, not just something we whip out when our children are misbehaving. Deuteronomy 6:6–7 encourages, "These commandments that I give you today are to be on your hearts. Impress them on your children. Talk about them when you sit at home and when you walk along the road, when you lie down and when you get up." In our children's presence we should take every opportunity to praise God, to seek him in every aspect of our lives, and to give him glory in all circumstances.

May our children recognize and respond to their need for Christ in everyday life as they witness us, their parents, doing the same.

Never Train in Anger

It is human nature to become angry. I dare say there are times when all parents struggle with anger when children disobey.

While anger is an emotion given to us by God, we are commanded in Ephesians 4:26, "In your anger do not sin." To discipline our children in anger is to sin against them and God. In James 1:20, we are told that disciplining in anger "does not produce the righteousness that God desires." On the contrary, we are encouraged in the first part of Galatians 6:1 to be wise in our parenting by being loving and gentle while correcting and instructing our children.

If you are angry, take a few minutes to pray and ask God to make your motives pure, enabling you to speak with wisdom and self-control before you instruct your children. Taking some time to stop and think about the impact of your words will eliminate the regret of those words later. Moms in particular deal with so much guilt and doubt. Satan loves for us to hurt our children with ill-spoken words in the heat of the moment so that he can smother us with guilt later. My friend Dori told me that she tries to avoid making hurtful, harmful comments to her children by reminding herself to "stop, think, and avoid regret" before she reproves them. Take the time you need if you are angry and tempted to lash out. You are ready to reprove your child biblically only when you are empowered by the Spirit to discipline with love and gently spoken words.

BE ENCOURAGED THAT IT IS NEVER TOO LATE

Perhaps while reading this book you've had moments of thinking, *I've not been training my children the way I should, and it's too late to start now. I've already blown it.* Please be encouraged that it is never too late to begin training your children in the ways of the Lord. I was a rebellious teenager when my parents came to know the Lord and began training me in accordance with his Word. The transition began with a humble apology that I will never forget. My daddy took my hand in his and asked me to forgive him for leaving Jesus and the Word of God out of our lives for so many years. He apologized for his neglect to train, instruct, and discipline me when I needed it. His humility impacted me greatly and began the fresh start of a new standard on the right foot.

You might begin your fresh start with your children the same way my daddy did. You might sit down with your children and ask their forgiveness if you have not been consistent in training them to obey. Explain that you love them too much to allow them to disobey. Clearly communicate the new standard of obedience in that they are to follow your instructions "all the way, right away, and with a joyful heart." Follow through with consequences when they do not comply with the new standard so as to avoid the confusion of mixed signals. Ask God to give you wisdom and help you to be consistent, and he will. "If any of you lacks wisdom, you should ask God, who gives generously to all without finding fault, and it will be given to you" (James 1:5).

Let Go and Let God

We need to understand that even if we are perfect in our parenting (hypothetically, of course, as none are perfect), carefully instructing in accordance with God's Word and not disciplining in anger, our children still have a choice—a choice that we cannot make for them. We must do our part as parents, but we must also accept that we cannot make our children righteous. Only God can change our children's hearts. We are to point them to Christ by training them in accordance with his Word and leave the rest to him. The good news is that even when we do not see the fruit of our training, we can be certain that God's Word does not return void. In speaking of his holy Word, God says, "It will not return to me empty, but will accomplish what I desire and achieve the purpose for which I sent it" (Isa. 55:11). That is good news for parents.

Keep Your Priorities in Order

As busy, pulled-on, and often-overwhelmed parents, the best thing we can do for our children is to nurture our relationship with Jesus by prioritizing our time with him. Now, I must confess I don't always have my priorities in order. And when I don't, I always face consequences.

I learned a valuable and quite embarrassing lesson on the importance of keeping priorities in order after the construction of our new covered porch. Once the construction was complete, all obligations and responsibilities went out the window. I had spent weeks thrift-store shopping for unique treasures to hang and cozy furniture to arrange. The hammering was over, the tools put away, the debris was cleared, and the workers were gone. My time had come. While I needed to be preparing for a presentation I was to give at an out-of-town ladies' luncheon and packing for the overnight stay, all I could think about was organizing and decorating my highly anticipated, gorgeous new porch.

My husband repeatedly warned, "Baby, you can organize and decorate when you get back, but you need to be concentrating on your presentation and packing." Each time, I shrugged off his words of wisdom. *My porch, my porch, my porch.* Like a dog with a bone.

The consequence for my lack of prioritizing was not revealed until the next morning in the hotel room, one hour before I was to arrive at the event center to speak. As a result of hurried packing, I had forgotten my pants. I had the dressy top, the right shoes, but no pants. Standing over my suitcase in the casual shorts I had traveled in the night before, with my toothbrush sticking out of my mouth, I could feel my face pale and my heart rate double as I frantically searched through the contents. "Shelia!" I desperately whined around my toothbrush, "I forgot to pack my pants!" My travel companion and friend bolted out of the bathroom. "You forgot *what*?"

Fifteen minutes before I was to arrive, we found ourselves racing through Ross looking for pants. No luck. It was time to face the music, time to pay the piper, time to come to terms. I had no choice. I was going to speak in casual shorts at a ladies' luncheon. A fancy, *white tablecloth* ladies' luncheon.

Trying to bring a little lightheartedness to the situation, Sheila offered, "If it makes you feel any better, G, I forgot my hairspray." I quickly cut my eyes at her. "Don't even." The new motto of our friendship: at least you have pants.

A Christian's top priority should be spending time with God. No matter how many distractions surround us, how many people are vying for our attention, or how many goals we've set for the day, nothing is more important than fellowshipping with God. It is communion with God that prepares us to meet daily demands and opportunities with the mind-set of Christ. No one had more demands than Jesus, but before he went about his day, he sought the presence of his Father in heaven. Jesus knew the importance of spending time with the Father, so he modeled that priority for us. "Very early in the morning, while it was still dark, Jesus got up, left the house and went off to a solitary place, where he prayed" (Mark 1:35).

When we make time with God a priority, he enables us to view the tasks of the day, whether urgent or mundane, through the lens of the gospel. Our thoughts become more like his, which prepares and propels us to respond to our children and all issues of life productively, effectively, and with gospel-advancing purpose.

If day-to-day parenting, or day-to-day life in general, has us bogged down, stressed out, and uptight, it can be a sign that priorities need adjusting. Jesus said when we seek him first, everything else will fall into place. "But seek first his kingdom and his righteousness, and all these things will be given to you as well" (Matt. 6:33). How do we make time with God a priority? We make it a habit. Just as we schedule any appointment, we schedule time alone with God.

Granted, with small children around, especially infants and toddlers, having a scheduled time to spend alone with God may not always work out. Be flexible, yet diligent during this season. Different seasons of life call for different schedules. When I had one toddler and one infant who rose before daybreak, I had to adjust when I met with God. Later in the afternoon while one was napping and one was playing worked better at that time in my life. I also found that during that season, I often had to snack rather than feast on God's Word. Finding time to sit for more than a few minutes and meditate on God's Word was nearly impossible, so I kept my Bible open in the kitchen. Each time I passed by, I stopped to read a verse, then meditated and prayed over that verse as I went about my tasks. Prioritizing time in the Word and prayer in this way became a habit that still benefits and blesses me today. It led to a continual and intentional effort to practice the presence of God all day, rather than only at a designated time.

The priority of spending time reading God's Word and talking with him through prayer pleases him immensely, and it keeps us more in tune with his active involvement in our lives, which causes us to live in a more peaceful, secure state. We become more confident that all things, even the bad things, work together for our good and his purpose (Rom. 8:28). Through this confident faith, he empowers us to live in thankfulness to him regardless of circumstances.

I am living proof of the power of practicing his presence. On the days I fail to make time with God a priority, I tend to go down rabbit holes of negativity, refusing to see his good work in all things. On the days I do make time with God a priority, I find myself living in a state of thankfulness even in the midst of bad situations. When everything is going wrong, nothing is going my way, and I'm ready to throw in the towel, I can look to the heavens and, if for no other reason, say with gratitude, "Thank you, Jesus, at least I have pants."

A Note from Ginger

In conclusion, allow me to reiterate my heart. Please do not rely on this book as a how-to formula for being good parents who raise good kids. Our interim pastor Charles Carter once said, "Goodness without Christ is the worst kind of badness." It is a dangerous mentality to depend on the application of steps, even steps that are biblically based, in hopes of achieving parental success. There is no parental success, and there are no good parents or children, apart from Christ. Jesus is the power. Jesus is the source. Jesus is the good. I pray this book will not be a stumbling block that leads to self-reliant parenting, but merely a source of encouragement for teaching your children Scripture and their desperate need for Christ Jesus, our Lord.

My desire is to encourage parents to plant God's Holy Word into their children's hearts while acknowledging and living out of a total dependency on Christ. God promises that just as when we labor in a garden, we will reap what we sow (Gal. 6:7). Through the prompting and power of Jesus, let us keep on sowing the seeds of righteousness. And I can think of no garden as worthy of seed planting as the fertile soil of our children's hearts. To God be the glory.

ACKNOWLEDGMENTS

With all my heart, I'd like to thank:

My husband and best friend, Ronnie. Being your wife is the greatest blessing in my life. Thank you for your endless love, support, and encouragement. This book would not have happened without you. I love you more than you could possibly imagine.

My wonderful parents, Chuck and Bonnie Ferrell. Words cannot express how thankful I am for parents who not only provided a loving home that was full of joy, laughter, and the best of times, but who also set the contagious example of what it means to truly live in Christ.

My fantastic agent, Teresa Evenson. You praised my strengths, encouraged my weaknesses, and demanded my best. You helped put together a sharp proposal and got it in front of the right people. You forgave my pre-menopausal crying rampage and kept pushing for excellence in spite of my whining (I know, chapter 2). You've more than earned your keep. Thank you.

My amazingly gifted editor, Jessica Wong. The wisdom, insight, and talent you exhibit as an editor is well beyond your

Acknowledgments

years. I can't thank you enough for your hard work and the value you added to this book. Ten rounds with Rocky was well worth the prize. You. Are. Awesome.

My new friends at Nelson Books. I'm still pinching myself. Thank you for generously welcoming me into your family. I am beyond excited, humbled, and grateful for the opportunity to walk with you in the Great Commission. A dream come true.

My pre-publication readers. Many thanks to all of you who read through the manuscript and offered helpful input and suggestions: Dori Carpenter, Chuck and Bonnie Ferrell, Gina Ferrell, Wesley Ferrell, Alex Hubbard, Ronnie Hubbard, Lisa O'Quinn, Rebecca Ingram Powell, Candy Prater, Rick Riggall, Aaron Tripp, Meredith Wit, and Tricia Wit.

My friends at Shepherd Press. The wisdom I gained from the Christ-centered parenting books you offer not only influenced and shaped my own parenting, but also this book. Thank you for granting me the privilege of sharing what I have learned from you with others.

My Savior and Lord, Jesus Christ. Thank you for *everything*. To you be the glory, honor, and praise.

Notes

Chapter 1: I Know You Didn't Just Say That!

1. Stormie Omartian, *The Power of a Praying Parent* (Eugene, OR.: Harvest House Publishers, 1995), 26.
2. Ginger Hubbard, *Wise Words for Moms*, accessed June 21, 2017, http://www.gingerhubbard.com/shop/wise-words-for-moms/.

Chapter 3: Lying

1. James Patterson and Peter Kim, *The Day America Told the Truth* (Upper Saddle River, NJ: Prentice Hall Press, 1991).

Chapter 17: What's a Good Parent to Do?

1. Ginger Hubbard, *"Don't Make Me Count to Three!"* (Wapwallopen, PA: Shepherd Press, 2004).

Scripture References

Chapter 1: I Know You Didn't Just Say That!

- "For the mouth speaks what the heart is full of" (Matt. 12:34).
- "For all have sinned and fall short of the glory of God" (Rom. 3:23).
- "For it is from within, out of a person's heart, that evil thoughts come—sexual immorality, theft, murder, adultery, greed, malice, deceit, lewdness, envy, slander, arrogance and folly" (Mark 7:21–22).
- "Surely I was sinful at birth, sinful from the time my mother conceived me" (Ps. 51:5).
- "Bring them up in the training and instruction of the Lord" (Eph. 6:4).
- "Start children off on the way they should go" (Prov. 22:6).
- "A child left undisciplined disgraces its mother" (Prov. 29:15).
- "'For my thoughts are not your thoughts, neither are your ways my ways,' declares the Lord. 'As the heavens are

higher than the earth, so are my ways higher than your ways and my thoughts than your thoughts'" (Isa. 55:8–9).

- "The purposes of a person's heart are deep waters, but one who has insight draws them out" (Prov. 20:5).
- "All Scripture is God-breathed and is useful for teaching, rebuking, correcting and training in righteousness" (2 Tim. 3:16).
- "The word of God is alive and active. Sharper than any double-edged sword, it penetrates even to dividing soul and spirit, joints and marrow; it judges the thoughts and attitudes of the heart" (Heb. 4:12).
- We are provided with "everything we need for a godly life" (2 Peter 1:3).
- "If someone is caught in a sin, you who live by the Spirit should restore that person gently" (Gal. 6:1).
- "A gentle answer turns away wrath, but a harsh word stirs up anger" (Prov. 15:1).
- "The heart of the righteous weighs its answers, but the mouth of the wicked gushes evil" (Prov. 15:28).
- "Put off your old self, which is being corrupted by its deceitful desires; to be made new in the attitude of your minds; and to put on the new self, created to be like God in true righteousness and holiness" (Eph. 4:22–24).
- "God is faithful . . . when you are tempted, he will also provide a way out so that you can endure it" (1 Cor. 10:13).
- "Likewise, the tongue is a small part of the body, but it makes great boasts" (James 3:5).
- "No human being can tame the tongue" (v. 8).
- "So the law was our guardian until Christ came that we might be justified by faith" (Gal. 3:24).

Chapter 2: Whining

- We are "to say 'No' to ungodliness and worldly passions, and to live self-controlled, upright and godly lives in this present age" (Titus 2:12).
- "I have told you this so that my joy may be in you and that your joy may be complete" (John 15:11).
- "The word of God is alive and active. Sharper than any double-edged sword, it penetrates even to dividing soul and spirit, joints and marrow; it judges the thoughts and attitudes of the heart" (Heb. 4:12).
- "They exchanged the truth about God for a lie, and worshiped and served created things rather than the Creator—who is forever praised" (Rom. 1:25).
- God "richly provides us with everything for our enjoyment" (1 Tim. 6:17).
- "You shall not bow down to [idols] or worship them; for I, the Lord your God, am a jealous God" (Ex. 20:5).
- "Therefore, my dear friends, flee from idolatry" (1 Cor. 10:14).
- "Dear children, keep yourselves from idols" (1 John 5:21).

Chapter 3: Lying

- God lists a "lying tongue" second among the seven things he hates (Prov. 6:16–19).
- "I am the way and the truth and the life" (John 14:6).
- "You belong to your father, the devil, and you want to carry out your father's desires. When he lies, he speaks his native language, for he is a liar and the father of lies" (John 8:44).
- "Do not lie to each other" (Col. 3:9).
- "Each of you must put off falsehood and speak truthfully" (Eph. 4:25).

Scripture References

- The Lord "delights in people who are trustworthy" (Prov. 12:22).
- "He will bring to light what is hidden in darkness and will expose the motives of the heart" (1 Cor. 4:5).

Chapter 4: Tattling

- God lists "a person who stirs up conflict in his community" as one of the seven things he hates (Prov. 6:19).
- "Whoever gloats over disaster will not go unpunished" (Prov. 17:5).
- We are to "spur one another on toward love and good deeds" (Heb. 10:24).
- "Do not merely listen to the word, and so deceive yourselves. Do what it says" (James 1:22).
- "Let us not become weary in doing good, for at the proper time we will reap a harvest if we do not give up" (Gal. 6:9).
- "If your brother or sister sins, go and point out their fault, just between the two of you" (Matt. 18:15–16).
- "Be kind and compassionate to one another, forgiving each other, just as in Christ God forgave [us]" (Eph. 4:32).
- "A person's wisdom yields patience; it is to one's glory to overlook an offense" (Prov. 19:11).

Chapter 5: Defying

- "Children, obey your parents in the Lord, for this is right. 'Honor your father and mother'—which is the first commandment with a promise—'so that it may go well with you and that you may enjoy long life on the earth'" (Eph. 6:1–3).

- "Children, obey your parents in everything, for this pleases the Lord" (Col. 3:20).
- "For the word of God is alive and active. . . . It penetrates even to dividing soul and spirit, joints and marrow; it judges the thoughts and attitudes of the heart" (Heb. 4:12).

CHAPTER 6: MANIPULATING

- "Do not answer a fool according to his folly, or you will also be like him. Answer a fool as his folly deserves, that he not be wise in his own eyes" (Prov. 26:4–5 NASB).
- "Lord, don't you care that my sister has left me to do the work by myself? Tell her to help me!" "Martha, Martha . . . you are worried and upset about many things, but few things are needed—or indeed only one. Mary has chosen what is better, and it will not be taken away from her" (Luke 10:40–42).
- "John's baptism—where did it come from? Was it from heaven, or of human origin? . . . Neither will I tell you by what authority I am doing these things" (Matt. 21:25, 27).
- "Whoever loves pleasure will become poor" (Prov. 21:17).
- "Children, obey your parents in everything, for this pleases the Lord" (Col. 3:20).
- "The heart of the righteous weighs its answers, but the mouth of the wicked gushes evil" (Prov. 15:28).

CHAPTER 7: INTERRUPTING

- "Brothers and sisters, if someone is caught in a sin, you who live by the Spirit should restore that person gently. But watch yourselves, or you also may be tempted" (Gal. 6:1).

- "Love is patient, love is kind" (1 Cor. 13:4).
- "In humility value others above yourselves" (Phil. 2:3).

Chapter 8: Complaining

- "In all things [good and bad] God works for the good of those who love him, who have been called according to his purpose" (Rom. 8:28).
- "Give thanks in all circumstances; for this is God's will for [us] in Christ Jesus" (1 Thess. 5:18).
- "Whoever seeks good finds favor, but evil comes to one who searches for it" (Prov. 11:27).
- "Do everything without grumbling or arguing" (Phil. 2:14).
- "Take captive every thought to make it obedient to Christ" (2 Cor. 10:5).
- "Do not let any unwholesome talk come out of your mouths, but only what is helpful for building others up according to their needs, that it may benefit those who listen" (Eph. 4:29).
- "Rejoice always, pray continually, give thanks in all circumstances" (1 Thess. 5:16–18).
- "You intended to harm me, but God intended it for good" (Gen. 50:20).
- "Shall I not drink the cup the Father has given me?" (John 18:11).
- "I consider that our present sufferings are not worth comparing with the glory that will be revealed in us" (Rom. 8:18).
- "For we do not have a high priest who is unable to empathize with our weaknesses, but we have one who has been tempted in every way, just as we are—yet he did not sin" (Heb. 4:15).
- "Whoever can be trusted with very little can also be trusted

to your own interests but each of you to the interests of
others" (Phil 2:3–4).

- "Therefore each of you must put off falsehood and speak
  truthfully to your neighbor, for we are all members of one
  body" (Eph. 4:25).

- "Like a maniac shooting flaming arrows of death is one
  who deceives their neighbor and says, 'I was only joking!'"
  (Prov. 26:18–19).

- "All you need to say is simply 'Yes' or 'No'; anything beyond
  this comes from the evil one" (Matt. 5:37).

- "Speaking the truth in love, we will grow to become in
  every respect the mature body of him who is the head, that
  is, Christ" (Eph. 4:15).

- "Do to others what you would have them do to you" (Matt.
  7:12).

- "They follow their own evil desires; they boast about
  themselves and flatter others for their own advantage"
  (Jude 1:16).

- "They flatter with their lips but harbor deception in their
  hearts" (Ps. 12:2).

- "Not a word from their mouth can be trusted; their heart is
  filled with malice. Their throat is an open grave; with their
  tongues they tell lies" (Ps. 5:9).

- "For such people are not serving our Lord Christ, but their
  own appetites. By smooth talk and flattery they deceive the
  minds of naïve people" (Rom. 16:18).

- "And let us consider how we may spur one another on
  toward love and good deeds" (Heb. 10:24).

- "Your enemy the devil prowls around like a roaring lion
  looking for someone to devour" (1 Peter 5:8).

- "But encourage one another daily, as long as it is called 'Today,' so that none of you may be hardened by sin's deceitfulness" (Heb. 3:13).
- "I long to see you so that I may impart to you some spiritual gift to make you strong—that is, that you and I may be mutually encouraged by each other's faith" (Rom. 1:11–12).
- "Whoever mocks the poor shows contempt for their Maker" (Prov. 17:5).
- "Encourage one another and build each other up" (1 Thess. 5:11).

CHAPTER 11: AGGRAVATING

- "Make every effort to live in peace" (Heb. 12:14).
- "Those who promote peace find joy" (Prov. 12:20).
- "Love does not delight in evil" (1 Cor. 13:6).
- "Let us not become weary in doing good, for at the proper time we will reap a harvest if we do not give up" (Gal. 6:9).

CHAPTER 12: BRAGGING

- "As it is, you boast in your arrogant schemes. All such boasting is evil" (James 4:16).
- "Whoever has haughty eyes and a proud heart, I will not tolerate" (Ps. 101:5).
- "For all those who exalt themselves will be humbled" (Luke 18:14).
- "But when his heart became arrogant and hardened with pride, he was deposed from his royal throne and stripped of his glory" (Dan. 5:20).
- "So when you give to the needy, do not announce it with

trumpets, as the hypocrites do in the synagogues and on the streets, to be honored by others. Truly I tell you, they have received their reward in full" (Matt. 6:2).

- "And when you pray, do not be like the hypocrites, for they love to pray standing in the synagogues and on the street corners to be seen by others. Truly I tell you, they have received their reward in full" (Matt. 6:5).
- "Those who trust in themselves are fools, but those who walk in wisdom are kept safe" (Prov. 28:26).
- "All our righteous acts are like filthy rags" (Isa. 64:6).
- "For it is by grace you have been saved, through faith— and this is not from yourselves, it is the gift of God—not by works, so that no one can boast" (Eph. 2:8–9).
- "When pride comes, then comes disgrace, but with humility comes wisdom" (Prov. 11:2).
- "Do not think of yourself more highly than you ought" (Rom 12:3).
- "In humility value others above yourselves" (Phil 2:3).
- "Let someone else praise you, and not your own mouth; an outsider, and not your own lips" (Prov. 27:2).
- "A woman who fears the LORD is to be praised" (Prov. 31:30).
- "In the same way, let your light shine before others, that they may see your good deeds and glorify your Father in heaven" (Matt 5:16).
- "I have testimony weightier than that of John. For the works that the Father has given me to finish—the very works that I am doing—testify that the Father has sent me. And the Father who sent me has himself testified concerning me" (John 5:36–37).

- "This is my Son, whom I love; with him I am well pleased" (Matt. 3:17).
- "Well done, good and faithful servant" (25:21).

CHAPTER 13: ARGUING

- "A fool spurns a parent's discipline" (Prov. 15:5).
- "Folly is bound up in the heart of a child" (Prov. 22:15).
- "The way of fools seems right to them" (Prov. 12:15).
- "Fools despise wisdom and instruction" (Prov. 1:7).
- "Listen to advice and accept discipline" (Prov. 19:20).
- "Start children off on the way they should go, and even when they are old they will not turn from it" (Prov. 22:6).
- "A rod and a reprimand impart wisdom, but a child left undisciplined disgraces its mother" (Prov. 29:15).
- "Whoever spares the rod hates their children, but the one who loves their children is careful to discipline them" (Prov. 13:24).
- "The Lord disciplines the one he loves, and he chastens everyone he accepts as his son. Endure hardship as discipline; God is treating you as his children. For what children are not disciplined by their father? If you are not disciplined—and everyone undergoes discipline—then you are not legitimate, not true sons and daughters at all. Moreover, we have all had human fathers who disciplined us and we respected them for it. How much more should we submit to the Father of spirits and live! They disciplined us for a little while as they thought best; but God disciplines us for our good, in order that we may share in his holiness. No discipline seems pleasant at the time, but painful. Later

on, however, it produces a harvest of righteousness and peace for those who have been trained by it" (Heb. 12:6–11).

- "Therefore everyone who hears these words of mine and puts them into practice is like a wise man who built his house on the rock. The rain came down, the streams rose, and the winds blew and beat against that house; yet it did not fall, because it had its foundation on the rock. But everyone who hears these words of mine and does not put them into practice is like a foolish man who built his house on sand. The rain came down, the streams rose, and the winds blew and beat against that house, and it fell with a great crash" (Matt. 7:24–27).
- "Whoever listens to me will live in safety and be at ease, without fear of harm" (Prov. 1:33).
- "Whoever scorns instruction will pay for it, but whoever respects a command is rewarded" (Prov. 13:13).

CHAPTER 14: YELLING

- "Above all else, guard your heart, for everything you do flows from it" (Prov. 4:23).
- "Fools find no pleasure in understanding but delight in airing their own opinions" (Prov. 18:2).
- "To answer before listening—that is folly and shame" (Prov. 18:13).
- "The purposes of a person's heart are deep waters, but one who has insight draws them out" (Prov. 20:5).
- "Fools give full vent to their rage, but the wise bring calm in the end" (Prov. 29:11).
- "A fool is hotheaded yet feels secure. A quick-tempered person does foolish things" (Prov. 14:16–17).

- "An angry person stirs up conflict, and a hot-tempered person commits many sins" (Prov. 29:22).
- "Human anger does not produce the righteousness that God desires" (James 1:20).
- "Everyone should be quick to listen, slow to speak and slow to become angry" (James 1:19).
- "In your anger do not sin: Do not let the sun go down while you are still angry" (Eph. 4:26).
- "Get rid of all bitterness, rage and anger" (Eph. 4:31).

Chapter 15: Gossiping

- "For it is from within, out of a person's heart, that evil thoughts come—sexual immorality, theft, murder, adultery, greed, malice, deceit, lewdness, envy, slander, arrogance and folly. All these evils come from inside and defile a person" (Mark 7:21–23).
- "Let any one of you who is without sin be the first to throw a stone at her" (John 8:7).
- "Do not judge, or you too will be judged. For in the same way you judge others, you will be judged, and with the measure you use, it will be measured to you. Why do you look at the speck of sawdust in your brother's eye and pay no attention to the plank in your own eye? How can you say to your brother, 'Let me take the speck out of your eye,' when all the time there is a plank in your own eye? You hypocrite, first take the plank out of your own eye, and then you will see clearly to remove the speck from your brother's eye" (Matt. 7:1–5).
- "Brothers and sisters, do not slander one another. Anyone who speaks against a brother or sister or judges them speaks

against the law and judges it. When you judge the law, you are not keeping it, but sitting in judgment on it" (James 4:11).

- "For the entire law is fulfilled in keeping this one command: 'Love your neighbor as yourself'" (Gal. 5:14).
- "Love is patient, love is kind. It does not envy, it does not boast, it is not proud. It does not dishonor others, it is not self-seeking, it is not easily angered, it keeps no record of wrongs. Love does not delight in evil but rejoices with the truth. It always protects, always trusts, always hopes, always perseveres" (1 Cor. 13:4–7).
- "Do not go about spreading slander" (Lev. 19:16).
- "Whoever . . . spreads slander is a fool" (Prov. 10:18).
- "The words of a gossip are like choice morsels; they go down to the inmost parts" (Prov. 18:8).
- "[The tongue] corrupts the whole body, sets the whole course of one's life on fire, and is itself set on fire by hell" (James 3:6).
- "Those who speak rashly will come to ruin" (Prov. 13:3).
- "A perverse person stirs up conflict, and a gossip separates close friends" (Prov. 16:28).
- "A gossip betrays a confidence; so avoid anyone who talks too much" (Prov. 20:19).
- "Bad company corrupts good character" (1 Cor. 15:33).
- "The tongue has the power of life and death" (Prov. 18:21).
- "Do to others as you would have them do to you" (Luke 6:31).
- "You, therefore, have no excuse, you who pass judgment on someone else, for at whatever point you judge another, you are condemning yourself, because you who pass judgment do the same things" (Rom. 2:1).

- "Without wood a fire goes out; without a gossip a quarrel dies down" (Prov. 26:20).
- "If anyone speaks, they should do so as one who speaks the very words of God. If anyone serves, they should do so with the strength God provides, so that in all things God may be praised through Jesus Christ. To him be the glory and the power for ever and ever. Amen" (1 Peter 4:11).

CHAPTER 16: BICKERING

- "Where there is strife, there is pride" (Prov. 13:10).
- "A person's wisdom yields patience; it is to one's glory to overlook an offense" (Prov. 19:11).
- "Don't have anything to do with foolish and stupid arguments, because you know they produce quarrels" (2 Tim. 2:23).
- "If you bite and devour each other, watch out or you will be destroyed by each other" (Gal. 5:15).
- "Starting a quarrel is like breaching a dam; so drop the matter before a dispute breaks out" (Prov. 17:14).
- "Settle matters quickly" (Matt. 5:25).
- "Love is patient, love is kind. It does not envy, it does not boast, it is not proud. It does not dishonor others, it is not self-seeking, it is not easily angered, it keeps no record of wrongs. Love does not delight in evil but rejoices with the truth. It always protects, always trusts, always hopes, always perseveres" (1 Cor. 13:4–7).
- "Be completely humble and gentle; be patient, bearing with one another in love. Make every effort to keep the unity of the Spirit through the bond of peace" (Eph. 4:2–3).

- "Those who promote peace have joy" (Prov. 12:20).
- "How good and pleasant it is when God's people live together in unity" (Ps. 133:1).
- "Make every effort to do what leads to peace and to mutual edification" (Rom. 14:19).

CHAPTER 17: WHAT'S A GOOD PARENT TO DO?

- "All you need to say is simply 'Yes' or 'No'; anything beyond this comes from the evil one" (Matt. 5:37).
- "If the trumpet does not sound a clear call, who will get ready for battle?" (1 Cor. 14:8).
- "The heart of the righteous *weighs* its answers" (Prov. 15:28, emphasis added).
- "No discipline seems pleasant at the time, but painful. Later on, however, it produces a harvest of righteousness and peace for those who have been trained by it" (Heb. 12:11).
- "Let us not become weary in doing good, for at the proper time we will reap a harvest if we do not give up" (Gal. 6:9).
- "These commandments that I give you today are to be on your hearts. Impress them on your children. Talk about them when you sit at home and when you walk along the road, when you lie down and when you get up" (Deut. 6:6–7).
- "In your anger, do not sin" (Eph. 4:26).
- "Anger does not produce the righteousness that God desires" (James 1:20).
- "If any of you lacks wisdom, you should ask God, who gives generously to all without finding fault, and it will be given to you" (Prov. 1:5).
- "[My word] will not return to me empty, but will

accomplish what I desire and achieve the purpose for which I sent it" (Isa. 55:11).

- "Very early in the morning, while it was still dark, Jesus got up, left the house and went off to a solitary place, where he prayed" (Mark 1:35).
- "But seek first his kingdom and his righteousness, and all these things will be given to you as well" (Matt. 6:33).

ABOUT THE AUTHOR

Ginger Hubbard is a sought-after speaker, author, and award-winning writer. Best known for her popular book *"Don't Make Me Count to Three!"* and the *Wise Words for Moms* chart, she has spoken at hundreds of parenting conferences, moms' events, and homeschool conventions across the country.

Jesus-saved and Southern-raised, Ginger enjoys reading, writing, and spending time with her husband on Lake Martin, where they are forever honeymooning. Ginger is a veteran home-schooling mother of two fabulous children and stepmom to two much adored stepsons. When they are not traveling or on the lake, she and her husband, Ronnie, reside in Opelika, Alabama, where they enjoy working together from home.

★*

First of all, I'd like to say thank you so much for taking time to read *I Can't Believe You Just Said That!* It has truly been an honor to share this time with you. I wish I could give you a warm Southern hug and tell you face-to-face that you are a great mom. How do I know you are a great mom? Because a great mom is always looking to nurture and train her children in the ways of the Lord, and I know you purchased this book with a heart to do just that. Now that we've connected, I'm not ready to say good-bye, so I invite you to visit my website www.GingerHubbard.com where you can sign up to receive my encouraging blogs, fantastic giveaways, and see when I'll be speaking at a women's conference or moms' event near you. Until we can meet face-to-face, I would love to connect with you on a more day-to-day, personal level through Facebook @OfficialGingerHubbard and Instagram @ginger.hubbard. Hope to see you soon!

Blessings to you and your family,
Ginger